GW01466105

Neighbours in Space and Time

Grafton Architects at Sir John Soane's Museum

Edited by Grafton Architects and Louise Stewart

Published on the occasion of the exhibition
*Neighbours in Space and Time: Grafton
Architects at Sir John Soane's Museum*

19 October 2022 to 8 January 2023

Published in 2022 by
Sir John Soane's Museum
13 Lincoln's Inn Fields
London WC2A 3BP
+44 (0)20 7405 2107
www.soane.org

Texts © Sir John Soane's Museum
and the Authors
Design: Patrick Morrissey, Unlimited
Project Editor: Louise Stewart
and Grafton Architects
Picture Researcher: Nathan Emery
and Erin McKellar
Proofreaders: Sue Palmer, Erin McKellar
and Helen Dorey
Printed and bound in the UK

British Library Cataloguing in Publication Data
A catalogue record for this book is available from
the British Library

ISBN 978-1-9996932-7-5

Cover image: Contextual elevation of the
Marshall Building onto Lincoln's Inn Fields.
Grafton Architects.

Contents

Foreword

It is a great pleasure to welcome the opening of *Neighbours in Space and Time: Grafton Architects at Sir John Soane's Museum*. In development for over three years, the exhibition highlights the affinities between Sir John Soane's Museum and its newest companion in Lincoln's Inn Fields, the Marshall Building for the London School of Economics and Political Science. At first glance, there may seem to be little connection between the two buildings, but if we look beyond the difference in stylistic language, we can find points of comparison that show how vital John Soane's approach to architecture remains today. Above all, there is a sensitivity to light and texture, especially in the use of Portland stone, that constitutes a link across our communal square and across two centuries between Soane and the gifted team of contemporary Irish architects who trace their inspiration from him.

Grafton were drawn to the example of John Soane as an innovator, an architect who was interested in new technologies available in his day. Research in the Soane

Museum's drawings collection allowed Grafton to explore these parallels further, particularly the synergy between Soane's progress drawings, which were an innovation in his day, and site photographs of the Marshall Building, which are paired in the book and exhibition. Other paired drawings show parallel concerns in working with particular materials, and a focus on the human dimension of buildings, emphasising ways in which Soane and Grafton share a tradition of craftsmanship.

The distinguished authors who have contributed to this volume underscore the vitality of the links between Sir John Soane's Museum and the work of Grafton. Above all, the importance of drawings as part of the creative process is reaffirmed by this catalogue, which is unusual in that it also functions as a sketchbook. We hope that the book also becomes a space for creativity inspired by these two buildings and the wider context of Lincoln's Inn Fields.

Grafton have established a reputation for creating spaces for learning, debate, and creativity, which is what

John Soane did with his Museum. With this exhibition and volume, we welcome the Marshall Building as part of the public forum that is Lincoln's Inn Fields.

This publication, and indeed the exhibition that it celebrates, have only been made possible thanks to support of a group of generous contributors, many of whom have had direct involvement in the construction of the LSE Marshall Building. We're sincerely grateful to Culture Ireland, London School of Economics and Political Science – Estates Division, Mace, Techrete UK & Ireland LTD, as well as donors who wish to remain anonymous.

Bruce Boucher
Deborah Loeb Brice Director,
Sir John Soane's Museum
London, July 2022

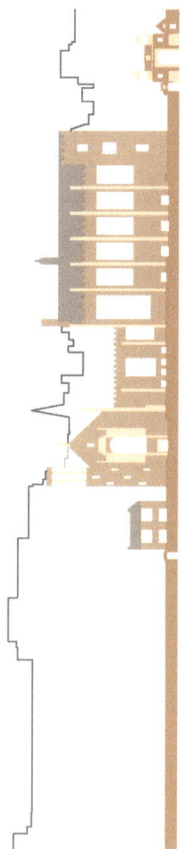

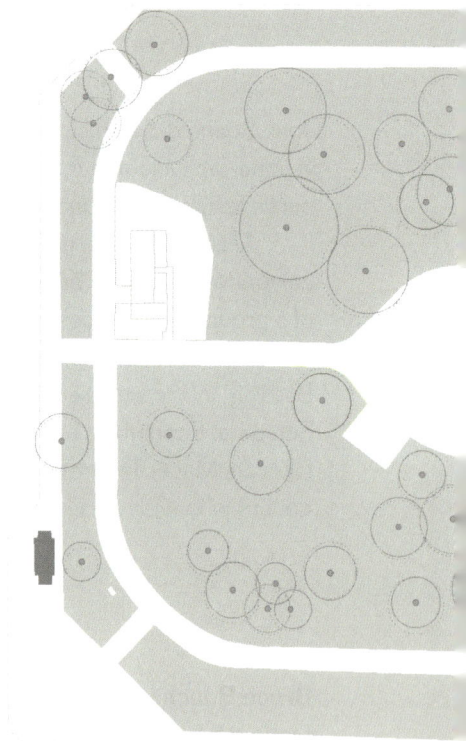

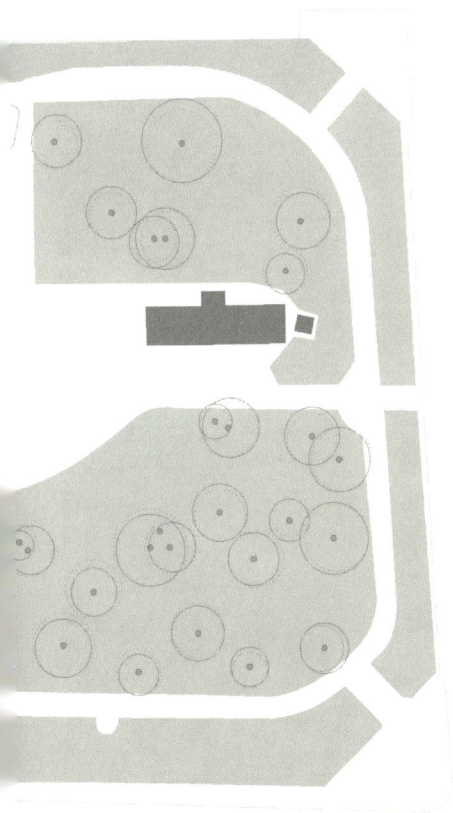

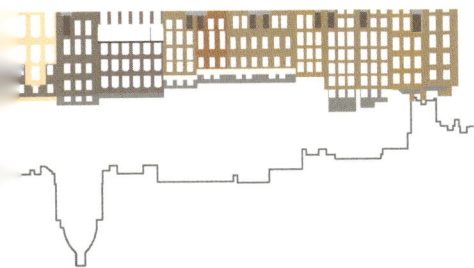

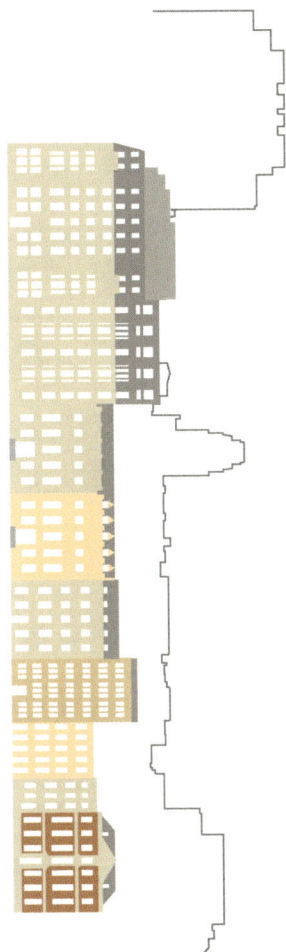

Neighbours in Space and Time
Grafton Architects

As practicing architects in the 21st century, it is wonderful
to be reminded and to realise, yet again, that the strength of
a great city is that it continues to be itself. In this exhibition,
two buildings across the same London square engage in
a spatial dialogue, where a north surface and a new south
surface continue to enclose a historic, shared public space.

Previous spread: Fold-out elevation of
Lincoln's Inn Fields. Grafton Architects.

Opposite: Site Plan of Lincoln's Inn Fields and
surrounds, with the Marshall Building, Sir John
Soane's Museum and Lincoln's Inn Chapel
highlighted. Grafton Architects.

Contextual elevation of the Marshall Building
onto Lincoln's Inn Fields. Grafton Architects.

Light in the City

Deep in the built grain of London, Sir John Soane carves and manipulates cuts in roofscapes, façades and courtyards. His architectural ability transforms buildings into perforated vessels where light pours in with the exact measure that the Master has mulled over and decided upon: zenithal light, side light, reflected light. Sometimes, like his close friend, the artist J M W Turner, he dips his brush into colour and transforms clear glass – a primrose yellow cheerily enriches a grey London day.

In describing the London of Soane's time, Jonathan Hill writes that 'Black rain fell on the city. Pollution coated yellow bricks, corroded stones and metals, killed trees and flowers, stained clothes and furnishings, and caught in eyes, throats and lungs, making streets and squares at times unbearable.'[1] Considering the environmental conditions of Soane's London, transforming dull light by focused intensity and colour takes on a new meaning.

1. Jonathan Hill, 'The weather in the architecture: Soane, Turner and the 'Big Smoke', *The Journal of Architecture*, Volume 14, Number 3, 2009, pp.361-376.

Opposite top: Frank Copland, Section through Sir John Soane's Museum and Breakfast Room, 1817. © Sir John Soane's Museum, London. Photograph by Geremy Butler.

Opposite bottom: The Breakfast Room looking North. © Sir John Soane's Museum, London. Photograph by Gareth Gardner.

Ancient Light

Above the entrance to a passage tomb at Newgrange, Co. Louth, Ireland, there is an opening called a roof-box. Its purpose is to allow sunlight to penetrate a chamber on the shortest days of the year around 21st December: the winter solstice. At dawn on a clear day, a narrow beam of sunlight penetrates the roof-box and reaches the floor of this man-made tunnel-like chamber, gradually extending to the rear of the space. As the sun rises higher, the tapped beam widens, so that the whole chamber becomes dramatically illuminated. This event lasts for 17 minutes.

The accuracy of this sunlight-catching device is remarkable, considering that it was built over 5,000 years ago – 500 years before the Great Pyramid of Giza in Egypt and 1,000 years before Stonehenge, in Wiltshire, England.

Above: Sunlight in the passage tomb at Newgrange, © Photographic Archive, National Monuments Service, Government of Ireland.

All this human, intelligent observation and labour was to celebrate and to 'capture' light. We refer to Newgrange here because, in the work of Sir John Soane, he continues this human honouring, celebration and 'capturing' of light.

When we began thinking deeply about our competition entry for the proposed new Paul Marshall Building for the London School of Economics and Political Science, one of the most important aspects for us was that the site for the new building was across Lincoln's Inn Fields from the wonderful Sir John Soane's Museum. This museum is a unique place, which we had gravitated to whenever a spare moment in London allowed. The experience of Sir John Soane's spaces confirms the true meaning of architecture: where each one of us is enveloped in space, activated by light.

Above: The roof-box admits sunlight to the passage tomb at Newgrange, © Photographic Archive, National Monuments Service, Government of Ireland.

Mastery of Light and Section

It is Sir John Soane's mastery of light and section that we most admire. His extraordinary control transforms spaces; tiny spaces can become magnified volumes; layered views with light draw you into a spatial matrix.

The Marshall Building has a 55-metre façade facing Lincoln's Inn Fields – a façade that faces north. In this location on the earth (51.570 degrees North, 0.1170 West) north-facing façades, because they are mostly in shadow, tend to appear sombre and cold. We manipulated the plan to create voids to allow south light to come through the north screen. We angled deep fins on the north façade screen to catch afternoon western sunlight, to bounce this warm light onto their surfaces, animating the 'lantern' façade.

Opposite: J M Gandy, The Monk's Parlour looking east on Aug. 16 1825. © Sir John Soane's Museum, London. Photograph by Geremy Butler.

Above: North façade, the Marshall Building. Photograph by Ed Reeve.

Light in Bocconi

In our Bocconi Building in Milan, Italy, we discovered that light 'desolves' structure. Zenithal light, side light, clerestory light, reflected light: all work together to give the illusion that the enormous concrete structures, including beams spanning 25 metres, resting on 3.6 metre-wide twin diaphragm walls, melt when light touches their surfaces. We also learnt that light bounces and tumbles down 5 metres – and more – 9 metres below ground, when held by the beautiful, white reflective quality of *Bianca Lasa* marble.

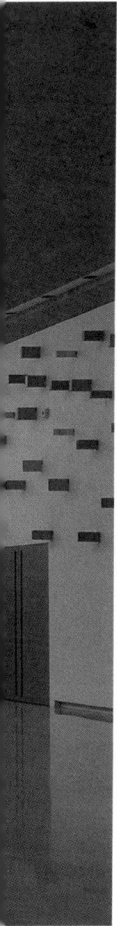

Above: View of Undercroft, Bocconi University, Grafton Architects. Photograph by Alice Clancy.

Ancient Stone: Soane Museum Façade

The façades of numbers 12 to 14 Lincoln's Inn Fields are of white brick with Portland stone dressing. Number 13 is distinguished by a Portland stone verandah or loggia projecting in front of the building line, which acts as an eye-catcher for people using the square. The two Coade stone figures at second-floor-level are versions of the caryatids at the Erectheion in Athens. Built into the piers between the windows are four Gothic pedestals from the 14th-century north front of Westminster Hall.[2]

2. *Sir John Soane's Museum: A Complete Description*, Sir John Soane's Museum, London, 2018, p.3.

Opposite: The façade of number 13 Lincoln's Inn Fields, © Sir John Soane's Museum, London. Photograph by Gareth Gardner.

Ancient Stone: The Marshall Building Entrance

Across Lincoln's Inn Fields, the stone used in the Marshall Building façade is also Portland stone – to be precise, it is a Portland Perryfield Shelly Whitbed, quarried in Perryfield Quarry, Isle of Portland, Dorset, England. It is classified as a Bioclastic limestone, has a slightly open texture and is described as a shelly stone. It is exceptionally durable due to its high shell content. The shell content and open texture result in a subtle variation across the appearance of the stone colour, tone and reflection.

This native Portland limestone has been extracted from the same quarries on the Dorset coast for centuries. We can imagine Sir John being fastidious about the qualities of the stone he chose for the façade of his Lincoln's Inn Fields home – the façade which would draw the eye of anyone entering the square from either the north-west or north-east corner.

Opposite: The entrance to the Marshall Building. Photograph by Ed Reeve.

Left: J M Gandy, View of the Study looking
north, 1822, detail. © Sir John Soane's Museum,
London. Photograph by Geremy Butler.
Right: View of seats integrated with balustrade
in the Courtyard of Santa Maria della Pace,
Rome. Designed by Donato Bramante. Petra
Nowack / Shutterstock.com.
Opposite: Design Drawing of Study Booths
for the Marshall Building, Grafton Architects.

The Little Study

There is something intimate about The Little Study in No. 13 Lincoln's Inn Fields. Somehow that space has a feeling that the Master Architect is still at his desk, at work here, thinking, testing ideas. This distinctive desk was tailor-made for the space, like the new desks which have been specially designed for quiet study in the Marshall Building's Great Hall. These were inspired by the carefully-scaled, stone seats in the upper cloister of the Church of Santa Maria della Pace, in Rome by the Italian architect and painter Donato Bramante.

Zenithal Light

The Soane Museum is an extraordinary example of how an architect can orchestrate light – the free and constant gift of Nature. In the Marshall Building, our tree-like columns reach up to the sky, drawing zenithal light to the lower levels.

Opposite: View of the *pasticcio* in the Monument Court from the Basement Ante-Room. © Dennis Gilbert/VIEW. Photograph by Dennis Gilbert.

Above: View from ground floor of 'Concrete Tree' stretching up to the underside of the third floor slab, the Marshall Building. © Dennis Gilbert/VIEW. Photograph by Dennis Gilbert.

Movement

Because of a diagonal shift of the party wall between Nos 12 and 13 Lincoln's Inn Fields, the curved stair in No. 13 has a geometry which allows it to widen at its north end as it rises up to access the North and South Drawing Rooms, increasing its grandeur and presence en-route to the rooms on the *piano nobile*. This sweeping, welcoming stair and the light provided through a skylight above, are part of Sir John Soane's thoughtful choreography for those ascending through the building.

The Marshall Building Spiral Staircase

In the Marshall Building, a 5 metre-radius helical stair in the Great Hall coils vertically up 7 metres through the warp and weft of the concrete structure. This corkscrew movement through the space reveals a panoramic view of the Great Hall in all directions, while at the same time bringing the vaulting beams close to the spectator. The space around this coiling stair compresses and then releases dramatically, revealing the four-pronged trees of the teaching levels as soon as one arrives at the first-floor level. As one walks down on this stair from the upper spaces, the stair encourages one to take the time to experience a sense of formal promenade. Interestingly, a person is also observed from the Great Hall in the act of ascending and descending the staircase.

Opposite: C J Richardson, View of the Entrance Hall looking north *c.*1834. © Sir John Soane's Museum, London. Photograph by Ardon Bar-Hama.

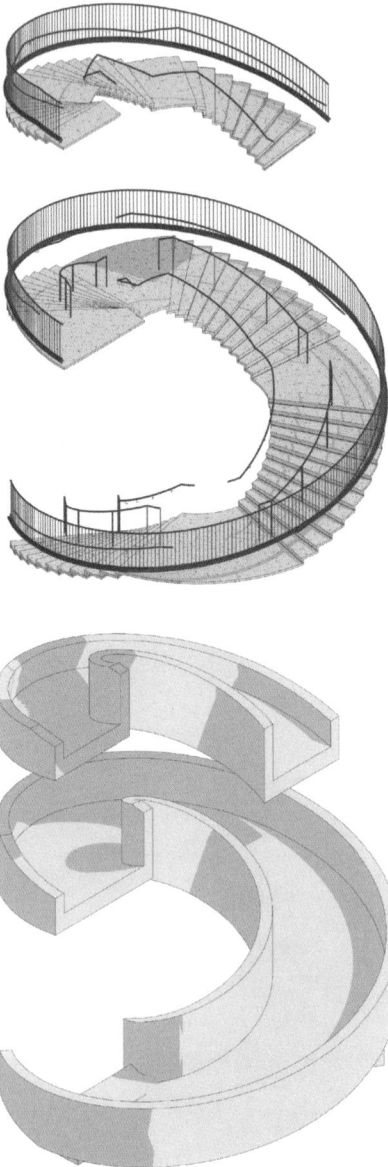

The simplicity of the curve of this staircase between ground and teaching levels is achieved by a low upstand concrete wall, together with a slender stainless-steel handrail. This creates the sensation of lightness that counterpoints the massive firmness of the concrete below. Rather than directly paralleling the helical curve of the concrete upstand, the stainless-steel railing is conceived as a shallow arched bow that wraps around the curved path of the stairs. This allows the height of the railing to be confined to positions only where it is required, relative to steps and landings. This bow maintains a smooth curve and is nearly imperceivable. It is necessary to the human experience, giving a feeling of safe containment, while at the same time allowing visual connection to the surrounding spaces as one ascends or descends.

Opposite: Exploded axonometric drawing
of the Marshall Building helical stair.
Grafton Architects.

View of helical stair, the Marshall Building.
Photograph by Ed Reeve.

The Marshall Building Entrance on Lincoln's Inn Fields

The conception of the ground-floor plan was to bridge the level change with a nearly imperceivable slope from Lincoln's Inn Fields to the London School of Economics campus. The diagonal cross-weave of the plan maximises the length across the site to minimise the steepness of the slope. This forms a common motif from the large scale to the small. The diagonal grain of the vaulting tree structures is echoed in the splayed incisions to the ground, in the notched alcoves of the entrances and even down to the minute scale of the detailing of the boundary railings to the north. Layers of splayed diagonal balusters convey a quality of depth and a sense of movement to the passer-by as one moves along their length. Shifting views and light in turn resonate with the precast concrete splays of the North façade.

View of forecourt, the Marshall Building.
Photograph by Nick Kane.

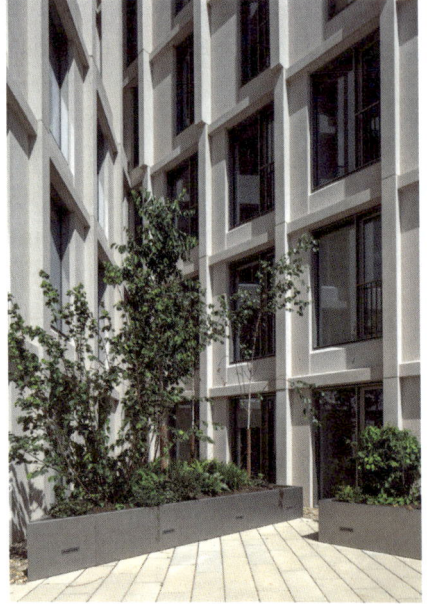

Above left: J M Gandy, The Soane family
having breakfast in the Breakfast Room,
No. 12 Lincoln's Inn Fields, November 1798.
© Sir John Soane's Museum, London.
Photograph by Geremy Butler.
Above right: View Terrace L03 the Marshall
Building. Photograph by Nick Kane.

Opposite: View of Terrace L08, the Marshall
Building. Photograph by Nick Kane.

Landscape

The vaulted ceiling of the No. 12 Breakfast Room in Sir John Soane's Museum is decorated with a painted design of honeysuckle and columbine on a trellis, as if the room was open to the sky like a pergola. Potted plants are visible outside the window.

Mediating between interior space and the city, enjoying the benefits of nature, the Marshall Building has thirteen terraces, eight of which have planting, some relating to the city, some relating to the sky.

The Imagined and The Real

It is always extraordinary to consider the power of human imagination. Spaces are invented, imagined by architects before they exist. Huge efforts go into making the imagined reality. Sketch drawings, perpectives and models trap ideas, allowing them to be tested before being translated into bricks and mortar, concrete and steel. The work of Sir John Soane was tested using the tools of the trade of his era: models, watercolour perspectives, detailed drawings.

Contemporary work follows more or less the same study routes, albeit sometimes using different tools; it also imagines a future that unfolds. As such, this shared practice of imagining, testing and translating buildings into reality facilitates a continuing dialogue between architects, across space and time.

Top: Competition stage rendering of the Great Hall at the Marshall Building, Grafton Architects. Bottom: View of the Great Hall, the Marshall Building. Photograph by Ed Reeve.

Neighbours in Space and Time:
A Visual Essay

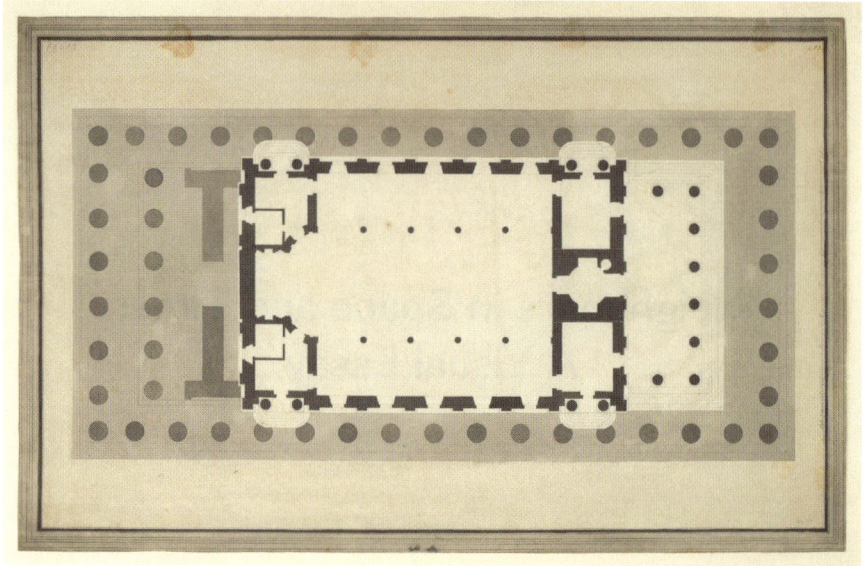

Comparative Scales: Plans

We have been intrigued by a series of drawings produced by Soane's office in which plans and sections of different buildings are overlaid on each other as a way of testing and comparing scale.

The vaulted undercroft of the seventeenth-century Lincoln's Inn Chapel inspired initial ideas for an open ground floor for the Marshall Building. The drawing on the right tests the scale of the plan of the chapel against the scale of the Great Hall.

Above: Soane Office, RA Lecture Drawing showing superimposed plans of the Parthenon, Athens & St Martin-in-the-Fields, London. © Sir John Soane's Museum, London. Photograph by Ardon Bar-Hama.

Opposite top: Plan of The Great Hall, the Marshall Building with Plan of Lincoln's Inn Chapel Overlaid. Grafton Architects. Opposite bottom: Lincoln's Inn Chapel Undercroft. Photograph by Steve Way.

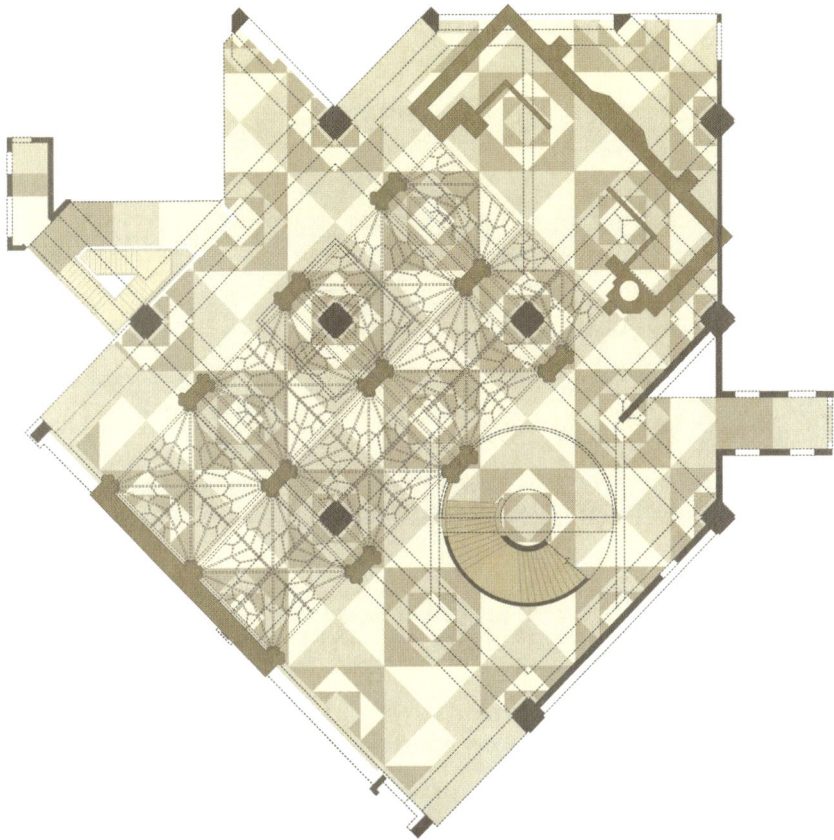

Comparative Scales: Sections

The section on the right continues the project of comparing the scale of the Marshall Building with that of Lincoln's Inn Chapel. On the left is a drawing produced for Soane comparing his own Accounts Office at the Bank of England with the 4th-century AD Basilica of Constantine, the largest structure in the Roman Forum, and the York Assembly Rooms, built in the 1730s.

Soane Office, RA Lecture Drawing showing comparative sections of the Basilica of Constantine, Rome, the Assembly Rooms at York & the Accountants' Office, Bank of England. © Sir John Soane's Museum, London. Photograph by Hugh Kelly.

Structural Section of the Marshall Building
with inset section of Lincoln's Inn Chapel.
Grafton Architects.

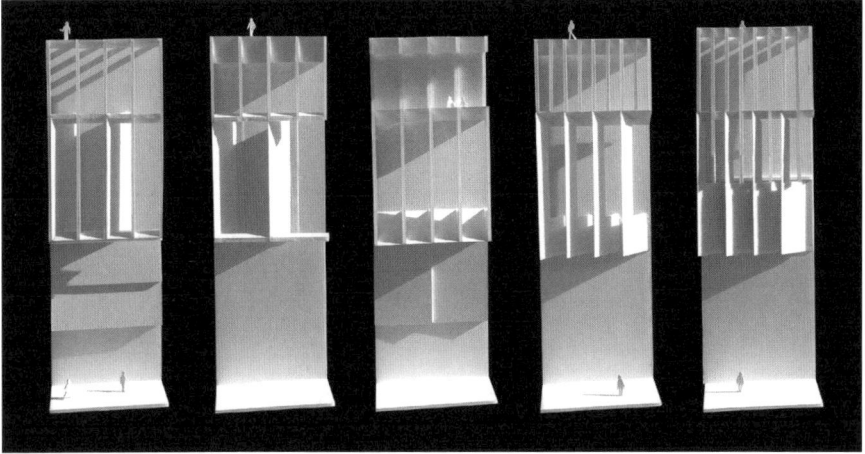

Layering – Adjusting Order

The Soane Museum's projecting loggia in Portland stone adds a layer of grandeur to the three terraced houses rebuilt by Soane during his lifetime. This layer modifies the proportions of the elevation, adjusting the reading of scale along the terrace.

At the Marshall Building a screen of precast concrete fins and beams span across the upper floor windows reflecting sunlight and providing shading from the west. This layer of elements spans across floors and results in a grander scale beyond that of the individual openings, creating an order that relates to the banded façades and porticoes of its neighbours.

Opposite: Model of the façade of No. 13 Lincoln's Inn Fields as originally built, designed by Sir John Soane, 1812. Photograph by Martin Charles.

Above: Light and shadow studies of the façade of the Marshall Building onto Lincoln's Inn Fields. Grafton Architects.

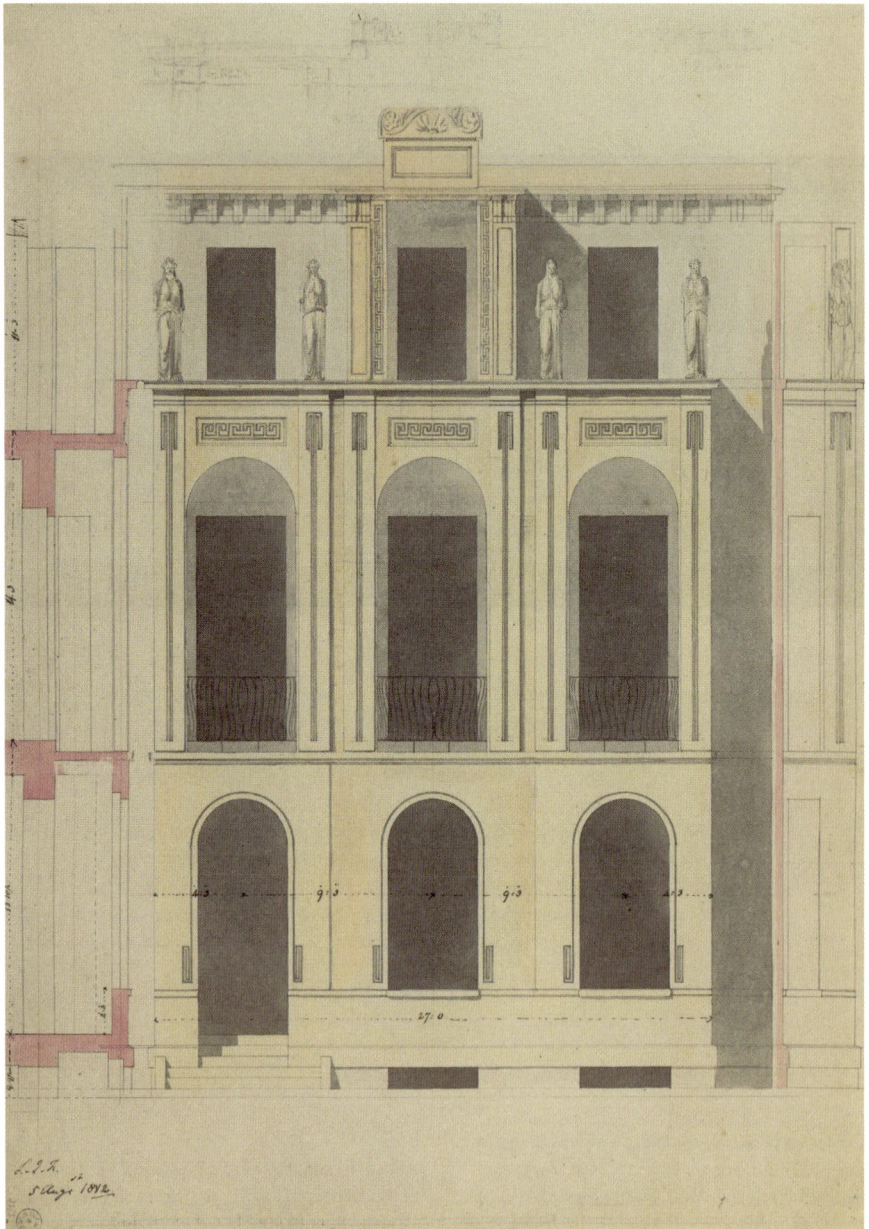

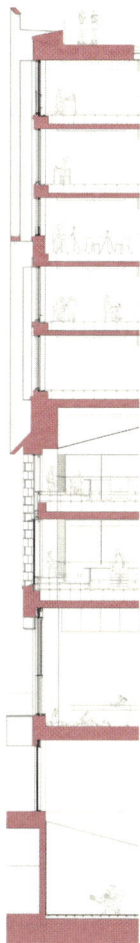

Opposite: Soane Office, Design elevation and sections for the façade of No. 13 Lincoln's Inn Fields, dated 5 Aug 1812. © Sir John Soane's Museum, London. Photograph by Ardon Bar-Hama.

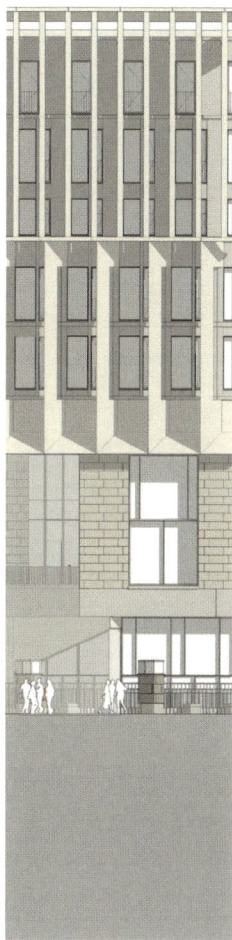

Above: Section and Elevation of the Marshall Building onto Lincoln's Inn Fields. Grafton Architects.

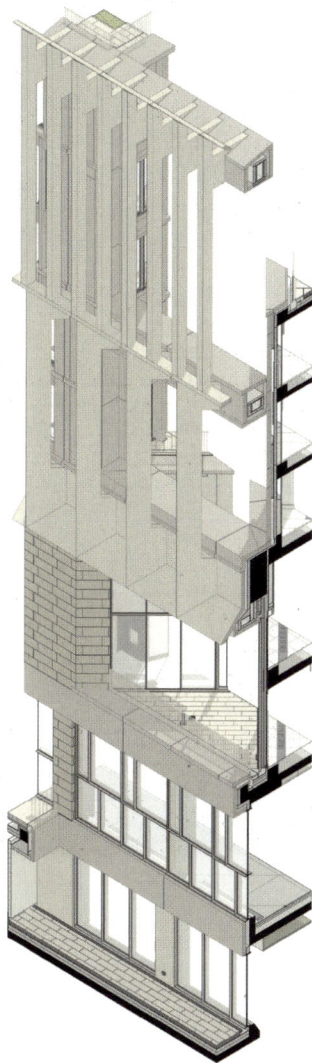

Opposite: J.M. Gandy, Perspective of the façade of No. 13 Lincoln's Inn Fields, as executed, c.1812. © Sir John Soane's Museum, London. Photograph by Ole Woldbye.

Above: Three-dimensional drawing of the façade of the Marshall Building onto Lincoln's Inn Fields. Grafton Architects.

Capturing Light
A Lidar scan of Sir John Soane's Museum, viewed in section captures two vertical shafts of roof-lit space.

The scan captures the cool colour of zenithal light in the Dome Area in contrast with the primrose yellow of the Breakfast Room and the soft warmth of the stairwell which is illuminated by a series of stained glass windows.

Using the same method we have captured the stepped atria of the Marshall Building where the structure branches out, tree-like, to pick up the structural loads bearing at the corners. This branching out also serves to reflect and bounce natural light from above, capturing it and making it visible.

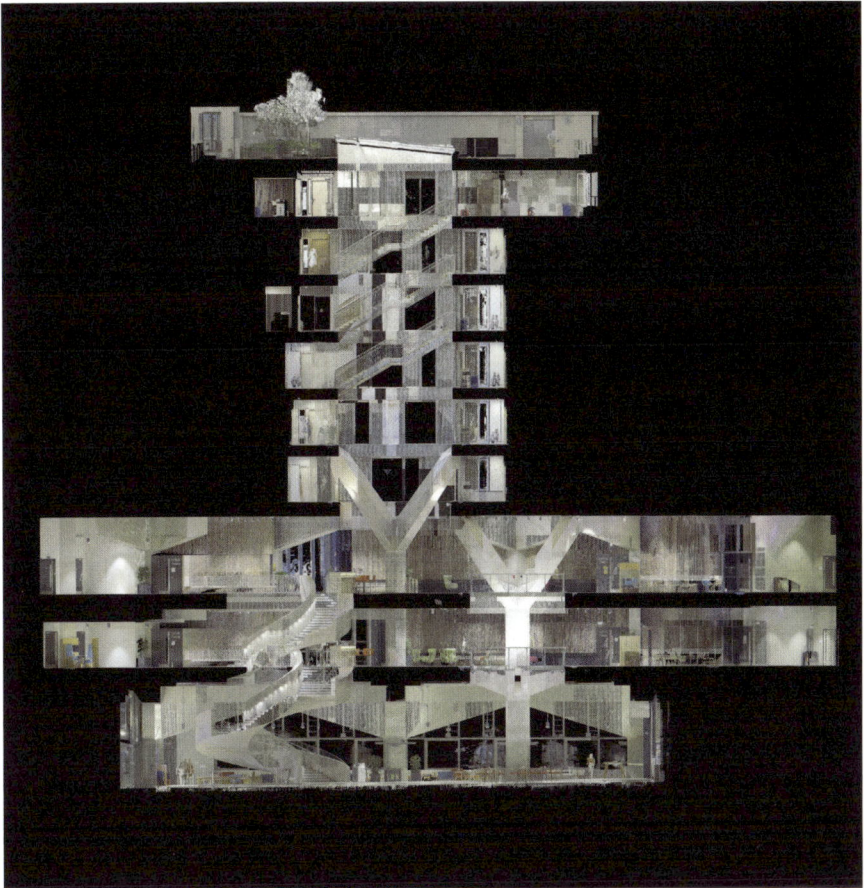

Opposite: Lidar scan of Sir John Soane's Museum. © ScanLAB Projects.

Above: Point Cloud Scan of the Marshall Building by Murphy Geospatial.

Above: George Bailey, Section through the Dome Area at 13 Lincoln's Inn Fields, looking East, 1810. © Sir John Soane's Museum, London. Photograph by Geremy Butler.

Opposite: Rendered section with inset plan and section of stepped atrium and 'luminous columns' at the Marshall Building, Grafton Architects.

Above: Soane Office, Design for an Ionic column, architrave, and balustrade at the base of the tower, St Peter's, Walworth, London, January 1823. © Sir John Soane's Museum, London. Photograph by Ardon Bar-Hama.

Opposite: Elevation and section details of precast cladding to parapet. Techrete – Precast Concrete Façade Designers and Manufacturers.

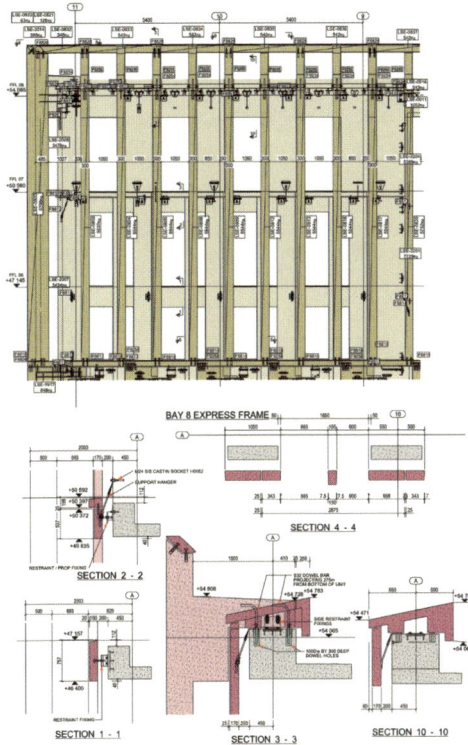

BAY 8 EXPRESS FRAME

SECTION 4 - 4

SECTION 2 - 2

SECTION 1 - 1

SECTION 3 - 3

SECTION 10 - 10

Shared Craft

St Peter's, Walworth was the first church Soane designed. The scale drawing on the left shows features of the exterior, including its Ionic columns of Portland stone and the open balustrade for the base of the tower, modelled here in light and shadow.

The top of the precast screen to the Marshall Building is modelled with sloped cappings, projecting drips and a series of open fins which catch the light of the sun passing over the roof of the building from the south. The drawing shown has been generated as a two-dimensional projection of a three-dimensional model of the precast façade system.

While the tools for design and drawing production have evolved, considerations hold across time, such as the level of detail required in drawings used for construction, as well as the practical need to shed water, capture light and craft something of beauty.

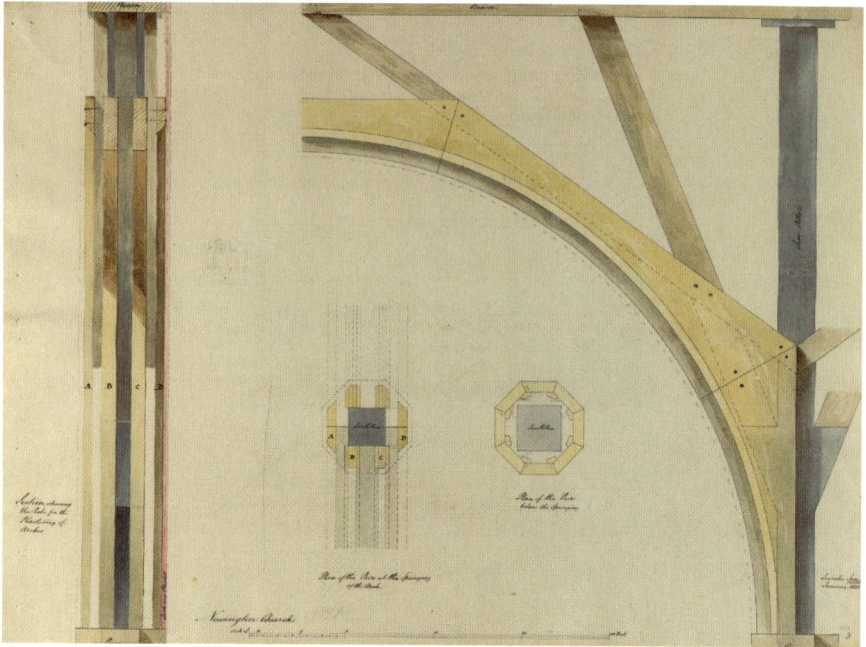

Shared craft

This pair of drawings both depict composite structures, one in iron and timber, the other in steel and concrete. While the construction industry and technology continues to evolve, the impetus to draw and describe elements in plan, section, elevation and axonometric remains.

Above: Soane Office, Design for the pier and ribs for arches, St Peter's, Walworth, London, January 1823. © Sir John Soane's Museum, London. Photograph by Ardon Bar-Hama.

Opposite: Drawing of concrete encased steel 'branch beams'. Grafton Architects with Model by Bourne Steel Inserted.

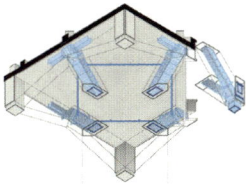
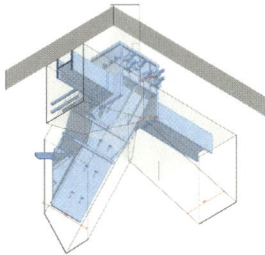
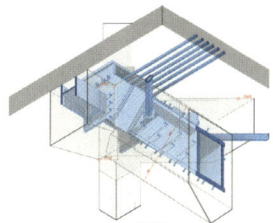
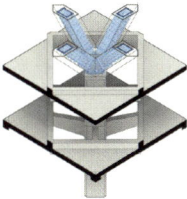
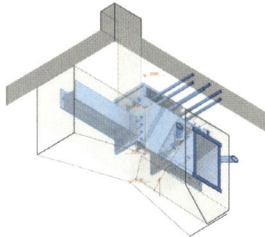
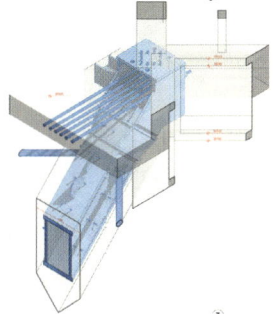
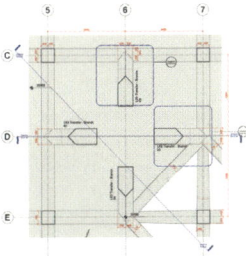
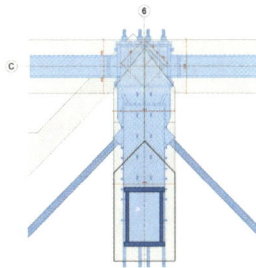
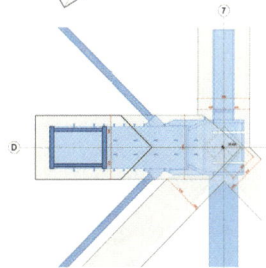

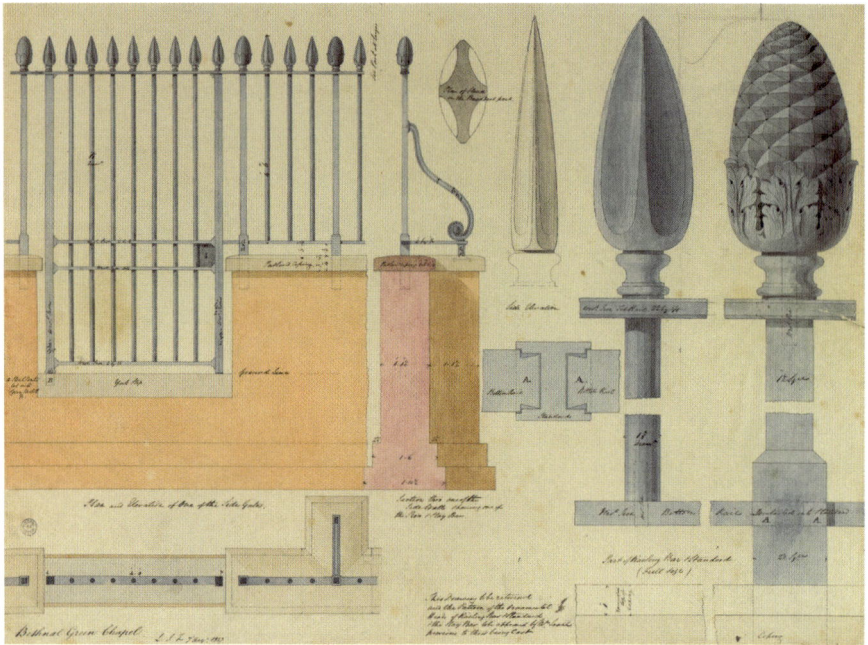

Shared craft

The need for protection and security continues across time, coupled with a desire to make 'soft barriers' that are open and transparent as well as being decorative and even playful while still deterring unwanted entry.

Railings designed by Soane for St John's Church, Bethnal Green feature simple bars in round and square profiles, topped with cast-iron 'finials' in arrowhead and pine cone motifs.

At the Marshall Building, steel flats are rotated at 45 degrees to echo the precast façade fins while allowing transparency to the passer by as they look along the oblique.

Above: Soane Office, Designs for the iron railings for St John's, Bethnal Green, London, 7 August 1827. © Sir John Soane's Museum, London. Photograph by Ardon Bar-Hama.

Opposite: Drawing of steel railings to Lincoln's Inn Fields, set into precast plinth. Grafton Architects.

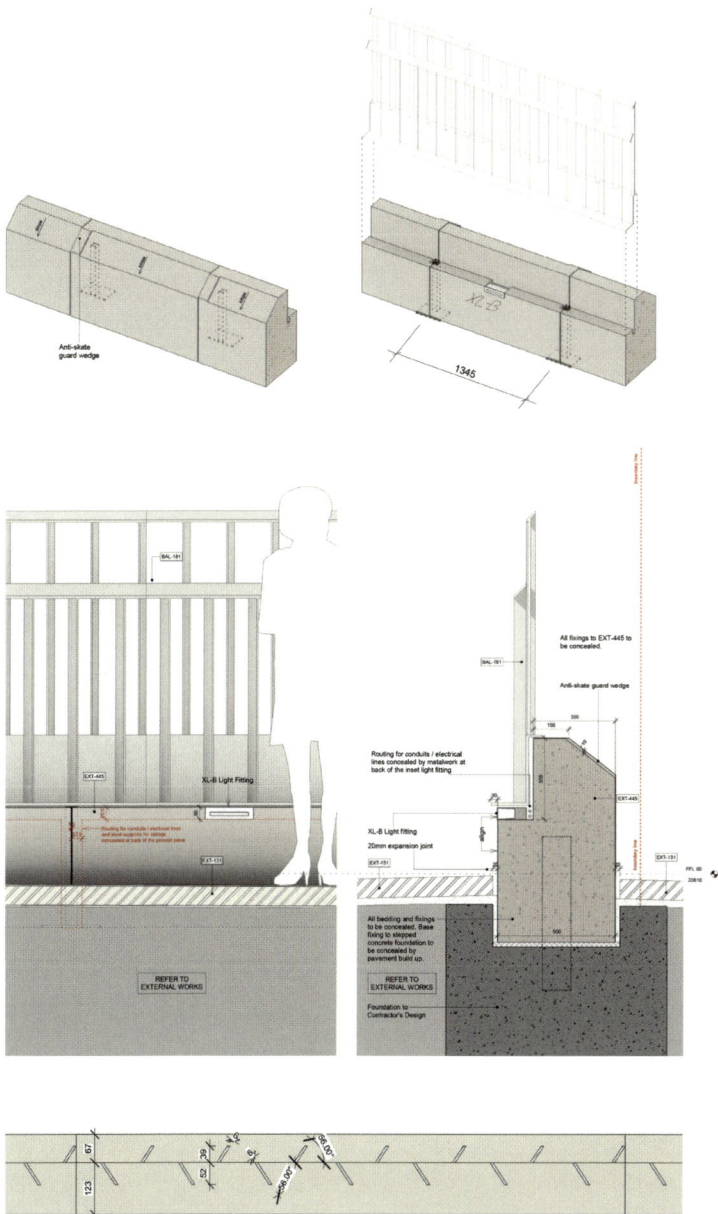

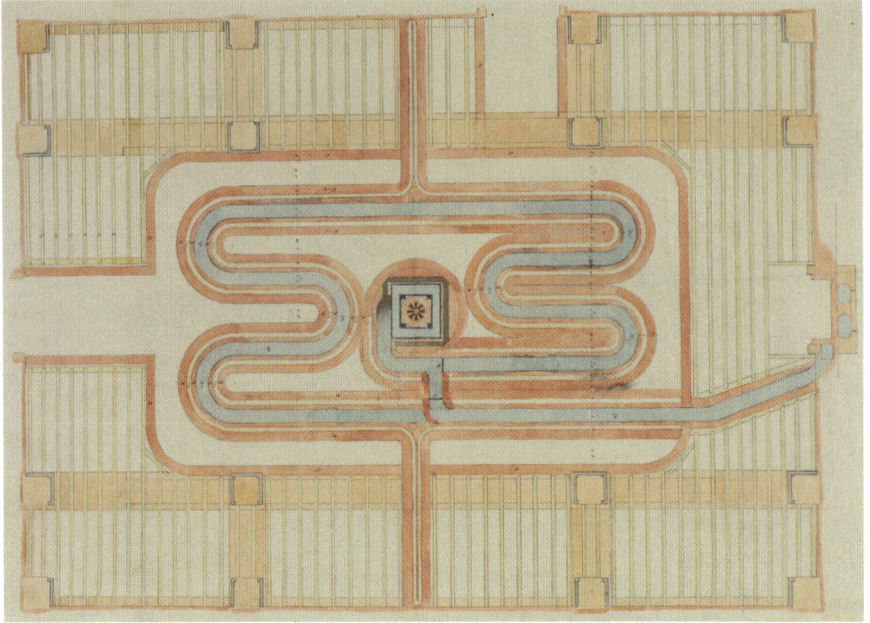

Comfort and Technology

This drawing shows a hypocaust system for heating the Stock Office in Soane's Bank of England. A central cellar firebox feeds hot air into a stove above and through a system of winding ducts beneath the flooring.

New heating technologies allowed Soane to imagine vast open and connected spaces that could be made comfortable through sophisticated systems discretely integrated into the fabric of the building.

The Great Hall at the Marshall building is designed as a 'buffer' zone between the external environment and the fully comfort-conditioned areas at upper and lower levels.

A target temperature of 18°C is achieved by use of simple systems such as a network of underfloor heating pipework, revolving doors and trench heaters and automatically opening windows for natural ventilation. The simplicity of the systems allows for maximum openness and flexibility of the space.

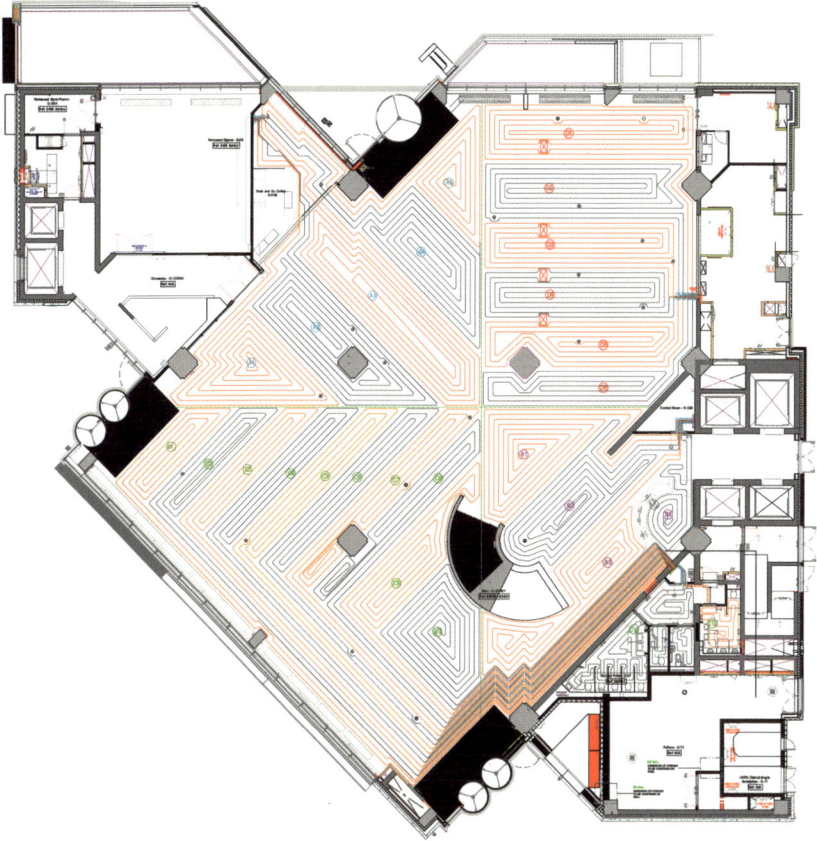

Opposite: Soane Offfice, Attributed to William Lodder or Charles Ebdon, design for hypocaust heating system for the Bank Stock Office, 1792. © Sir John Soane's Museum, London. Photograph by Hugh Kelly.

Above: Plan of Underfloor Heating System to the Great Hall at the Marshall Building. Lazenby Flooring for MACE.

Comfort and Technology

A long concrete bench, clad in polished terrazzo stretches along a series of sliding windows that open onto Portsmouth Street. A raised trench heater is positioned under the window to prevent draughts. Sockets integrated in the seat-back allow easy access to power, while projecting steel armatures conceal wireless internet routers and uplighters. The simple gesture of providing a seat to activate this edge is complemented by an ensemble of concealed and integrated technologies that allow for comfort and functionality.

Above: View of the Great Hall with Terrazzo Bench along Window, the Marshall Building. Photograph by Ed Reeve.

Opposite: Section of Terrazzo Bench along window to Portugal Street. Grafton Architects.

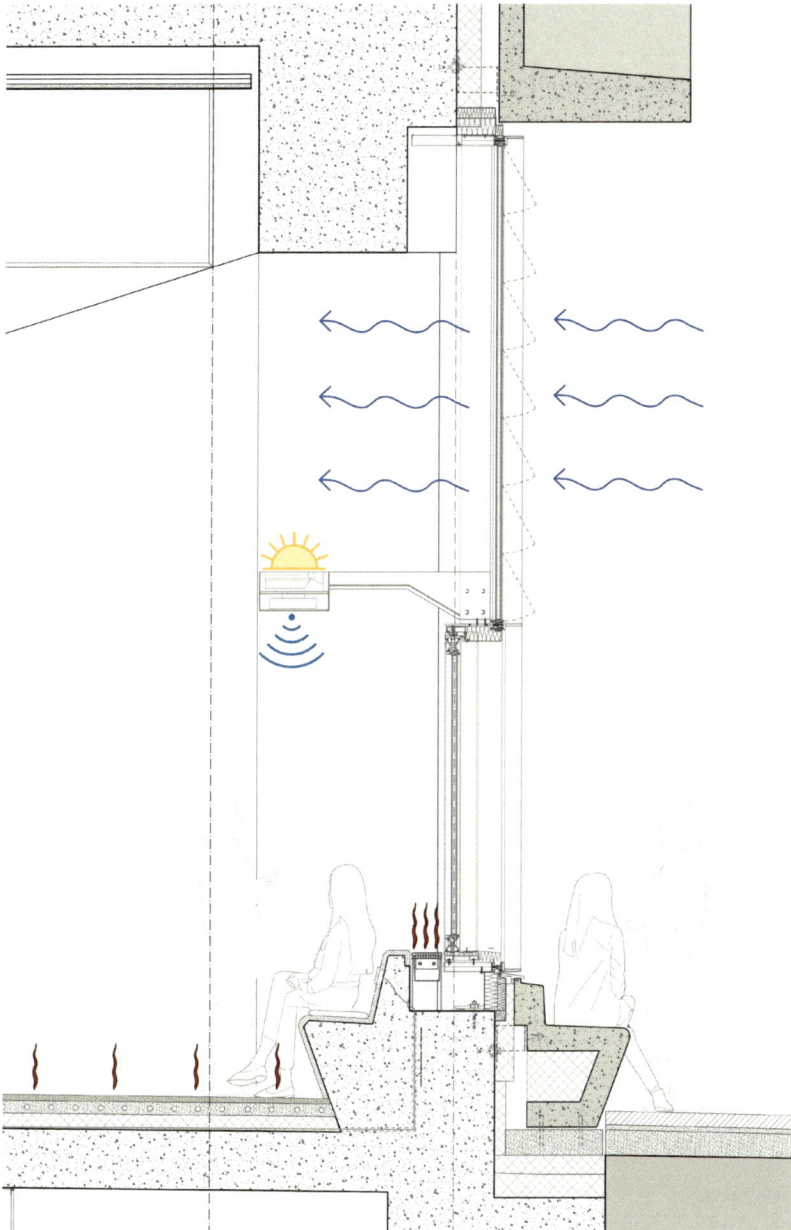

Neighbours in Space and Time

Coming into Being

Behind all construction is an invisible world of things unseen – temporary
structures to retain earth while walls are made; to support bricks while
arches are lain; to hold liquid concrete in place while cement cures.

   All structures come into being through the hands and minds of builders
and craftspeople. While technology advances to make new structures
possible and to make these processes safer, there are continuities across
time in how things imagined through drawings and images are brought into
being in the physical world.

Left: Soane Office, progress drawing showing
the Bank of England during the course of
construction, 1814-15. © Sir John Soane's
Museum, London. Photograph by Geremy Butler.

Right: View of 'Kingpost Props' to existing
retaining wall of the previous building on the
site. The Marshall Building. Photograph by
Grafton Architects.

Neighbours in Space and Time: A Visual Essay

Here, photographs of the Marshall Building under construction are juxtaposed with progress drawings showing the construction process of buildings in London designed by Soane. Seemingly unique among contemporary practices, the progress drawings were made by Soane's pupils from 1810. They provided an opportunity for the pupils to scrutinise building sites and the construction process.

Top left: Soane Office, progress drawing showing the Bank of England during the course of construction, 1814-15. © Sir John Soane's Museum, London. Photograph by Hugh Kelly. Bottom left: View of falsework to helical staircase, with inner and outer timber drum and CNC milled foam base. The Marshall Building. Photograph by Grafton Architects.

Top right: View of concrete branch beams connecting into 'tie-down' columns. The Marshall Building. Photograph by Grafton Architects. Bottom right: Soane Office, progress view showing the Old 4 Per Cent Office of the Bank of England taken down in 1821, d: 23rd August 1821. © Sir John Soane's Museum, London. Photograph by Ardon Bar-Hama.

Top left: Soane Office, progress drawing showing the Bank of England during the course of construction, 1814-15. © Sir John Soane's Museum, London. Photograph by Hugh Kelly.
Bottom left: Photograph taken from crane showing formwork to concrete branch beams – PERI steel formwork system with plywood lining. The Marshall Building. Photograph by Grafton Architects.

Top right: View of precast fins being installed by crane and MEWP (mobile elevated working platform). The Marshall Building. Photograph by Techrete.
Bottom right: Soane Office, progress drawing showing Dulwich Picture Gallery during the course of construction, 1812. © Sir John Soane's Museum, London. Photograph by Hugh Kelly.

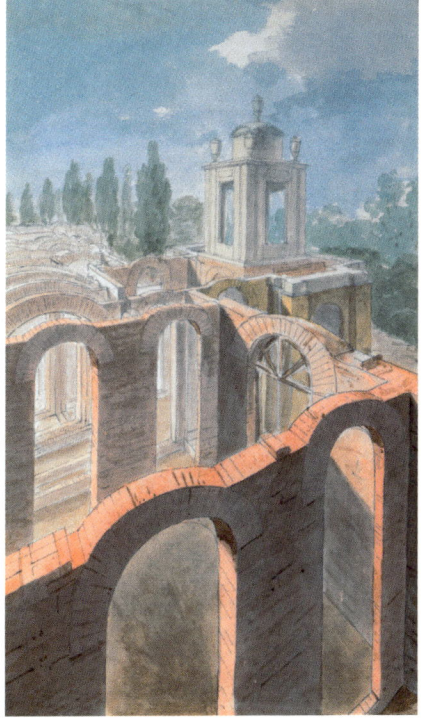

Left: Photograph taken from crane showing formwork to concrete branch beams – PERI steel formwork system with plywood lining. The Marshall Building. Photograph by MACE.

Right: Soane Office, progress drawing showing Dulwich Picture Gallery during the course of construction, 1812. © Sir John Soane's Museum, London. Photograph by Geremy Butler.

The Marshall Building Drawings

Structural Concept Image – Forest of Columns.
The Marshall Building, Grafton Architects.

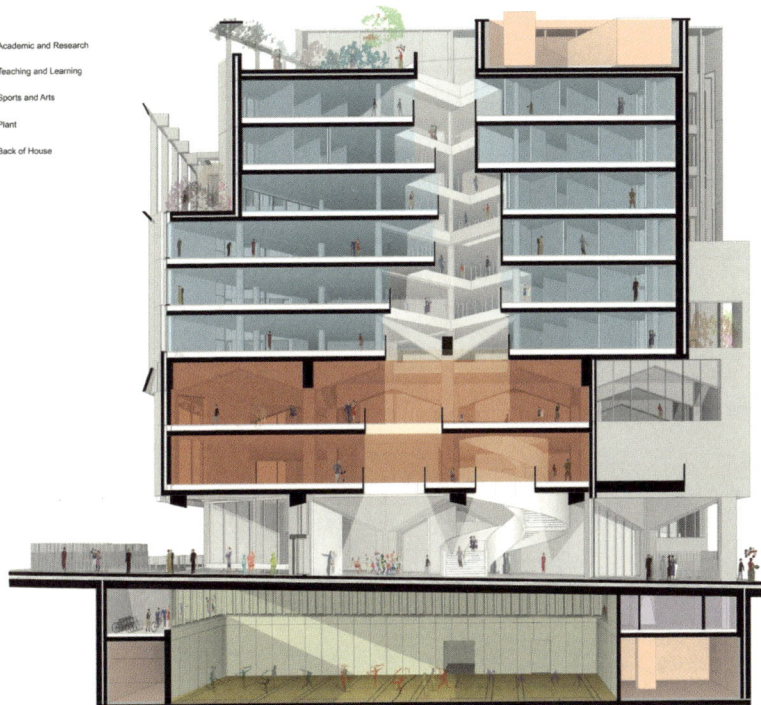

Academic and Research
Teaching and Learning
Sports and Arts
Plant
Back of House

Perspectival Section Diagram.
The Marshall Building, Grafton Architects.

Plan of Basement Level 1 – Sports and Arts.
The Marshall Building, Grafton Architects.

1   LSESU Reception
2   Squash Courts
3   Viewing Gallery
4   Sports Hall
5   Weights Room
6   Music Practice Suite
7   Bicycle Changing Facilitites
8   Bicycle Parking
9   Plant/Back of House
10 Staff Changing

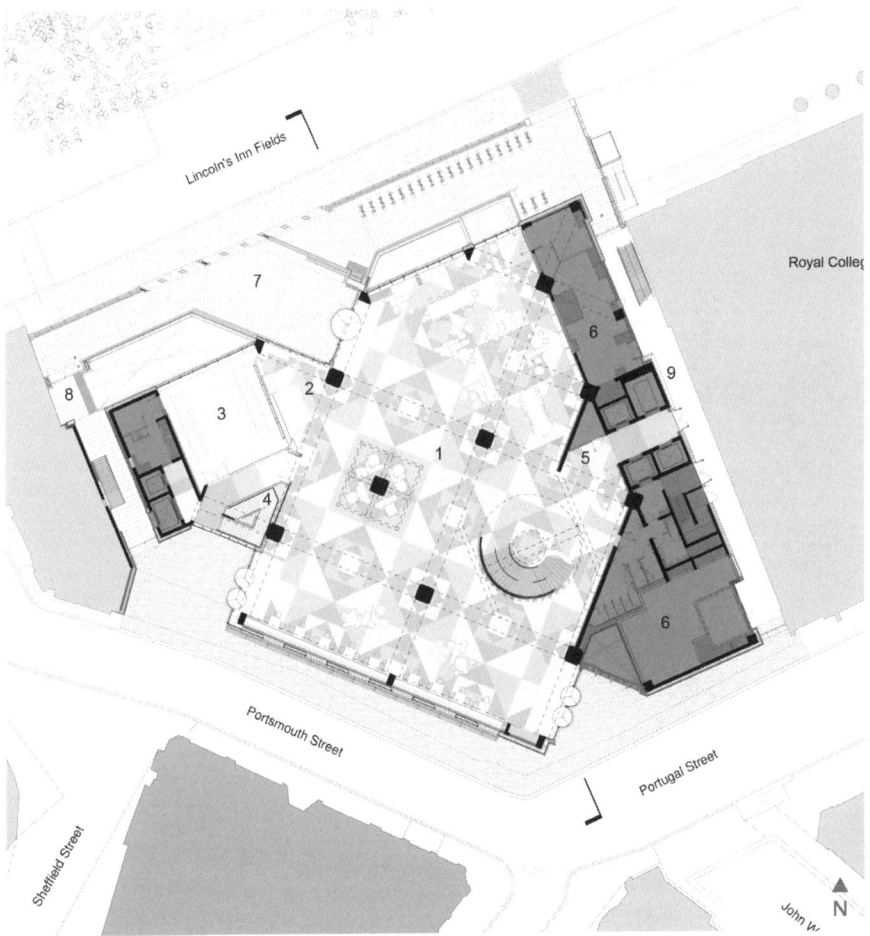

Plan of Ground Floor – The Great Hall.
The Marshall Building, Grafton Architects.

1 Great Hall
2 Cafe
3 Dance/Theatre Rehearsal
4 Stairs to Basement
5 Reception
6 Storage
7 Forecourt
8 Stairs to Bicyle Parking
9 Service Laneway

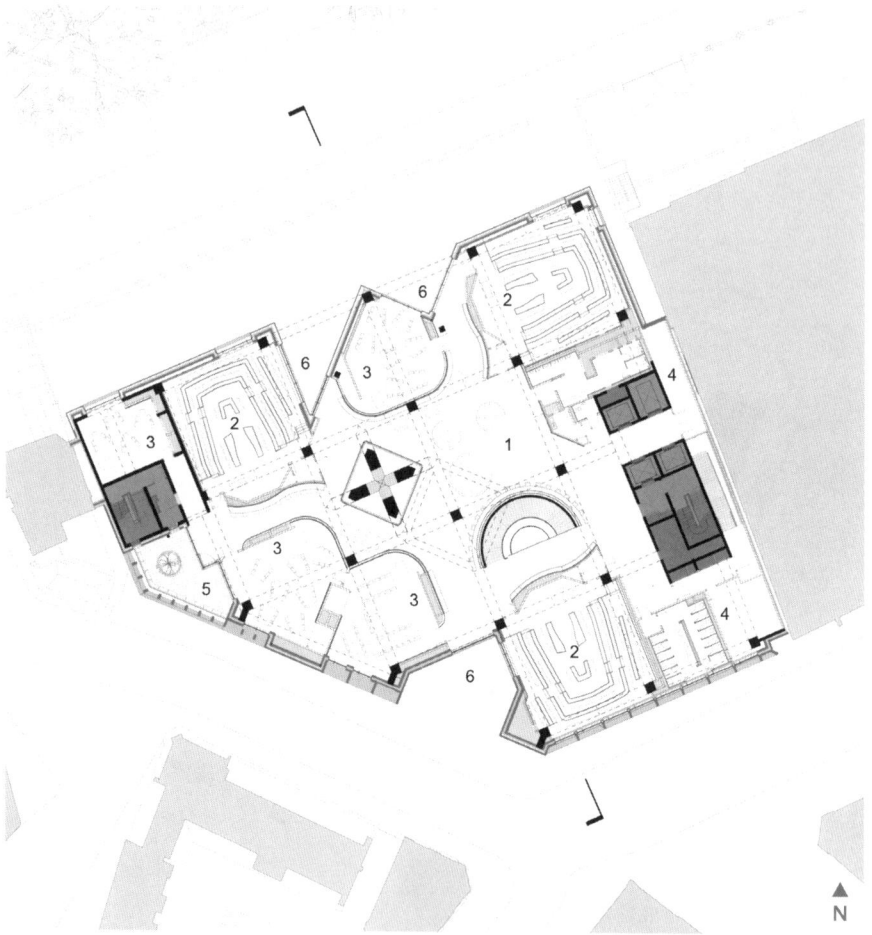

Plan of Level 2 – Teaching & Learning.
The Marshall Building, Grafton Architects.

1 Student Commons
2 Lecture Theatre
3 Classroom
4 Store
5 Terrace
6 Terrace below

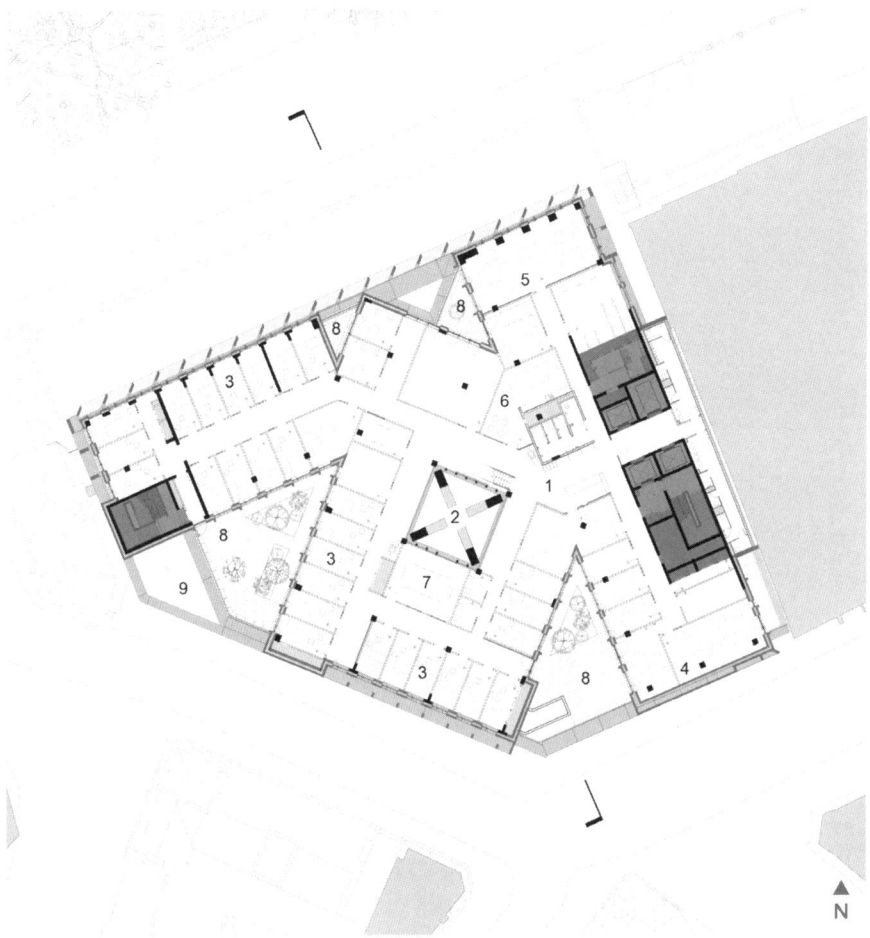

Plan of Level 3 – Academic Offices.
The Marshall Building, Grafton Architects.

1 Reception
2 Void to below
3 Academic Office
4 Grouped Office
5 PhD/MsC Study
6 Kitchen
7 Meeting Room
8 Terrace
9 Terrace below

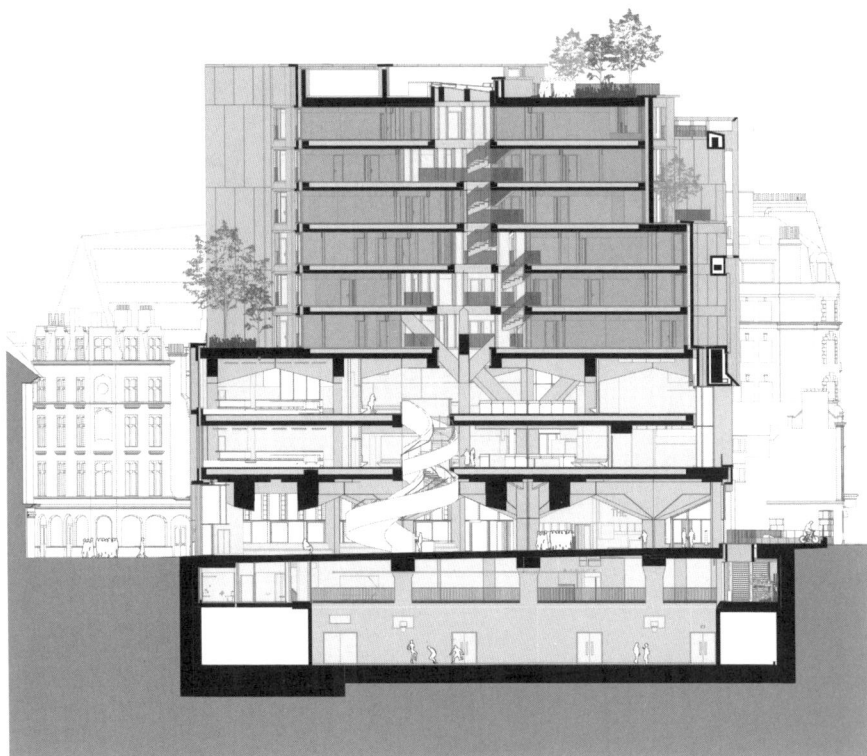

Above: Section looking west.
The Marshall Building, Grafton Architects.
Opposite top: Elevation to North.
The Marshall Building, Grafton Architects.
Opposite bottom: Elevation to South.
The Marshall Building, Grafton Architects.

The Marshall Building Drawings

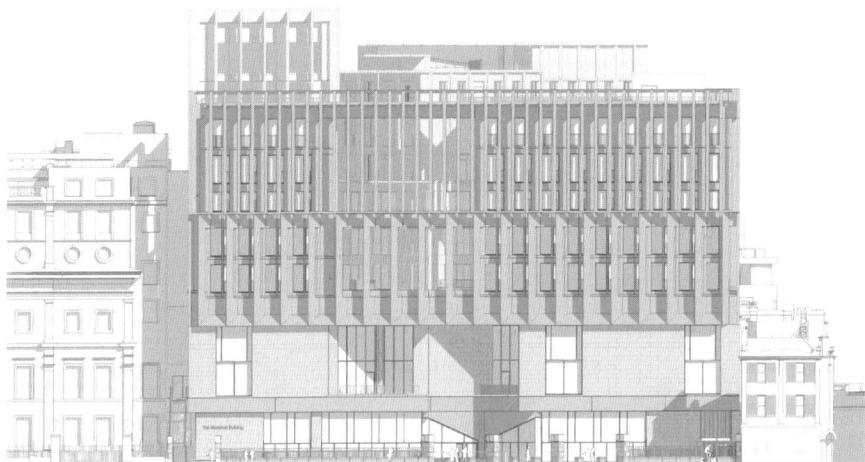

The LSE Marshall Building 2022
Kenneth Frampton

The LSE Marshall Building 2022
Kenneth Frampton

There is a structural expressivity in the mature work of
Grafton Architects which is totally absent in their early
career. This tectonic exuberance first emerges in their design
for the expansion of Bocconi University in Milan (2005-2009)
in which the brief required that the *aula magna* appear to
be as accessible to the general public as to the university.

This they achieved by cantilevering the main auditorium
over a large, clerestory-lit, subterranean foyer which was
directly visible from the sidewalk at grade. An even more
dramatic use of fair-faced, reinforced concrete construction
appears in their UTEC University in Lima, Peru (2011-2015)
comprising an eleven-storey skeleton frame supporting a
complex assembly of stepped classrooms and auditoria.

A corresponding use of wide-span cantilevered
form is evident in their newly completed Marshall Building
erected on a relatively cramped site in Lincoln's Inn
Fields, London, opposite the Soane Museum. Herein
wide-span cantilevers over the monumental space of the
ground floor, the so-called Great Hall, distantly echo in

Opposite top: Bocconi University, Milan, Italy.
Grafton Architects. Photograph by Paolo
Tonato, courtesy of Università Commerciale
Luigi Bocconi.

Opposite bottom: UTEC University Campus,
Lima, Peru. Grafton Architects. Photograph
by Iwan Bann.

their form the fan vaulting of the Gothic undercroft of Lincoln's Inn Chapel at the eastern end of the square.

This building evokes in its daring use of wide-span structure the pioneering concrete work of the distinguished British engineer Sir Owen Williams, particularly for his famous Boots Factory, Nottingham of 1932. However, where this pharmaceutical plant depended for its spatial rhythm on a grid of wide-span mushroom columns, the interior of the Great Hall in the Marshall Building stems from the overarching presence of heavy, reinforced concrete transfer trusses. These trusses on the ground floor ingeniously support a layer of lighter trusswork above, which, rotated through 45 degrees, serves to carry the nine-storey reinforced concrete skeleton frame above. Passing from 15-metre spans on the ground floor to 10-metre spans above, this ingenious 'piggy-back' construction is eventually brought down on to four, free-standing, square columns, completed by three attached columns on the periphery of the space, plus a single, so called 'tree' column that independently passes through a square void in the ceiling of the ground floor, so as to eventually support a light-well that extends through the entire building above.

This feature is paralleled on the ground floor by a helicoidal stair in concrete that, as a kind of *scala regia*, passes up through the ceiling of the ground floor to provide

Opposite top: Lincoln's Inn Chapel Undercroft. Photograph by Steve Way.

Opposite bottom: Boots Factory, Nottingham, UK. Owen Williams. Photograph by Sims & Co. RIBA Collections.

View of the Great Hall, the Marshall Building.
Photograph by Nick Kane.

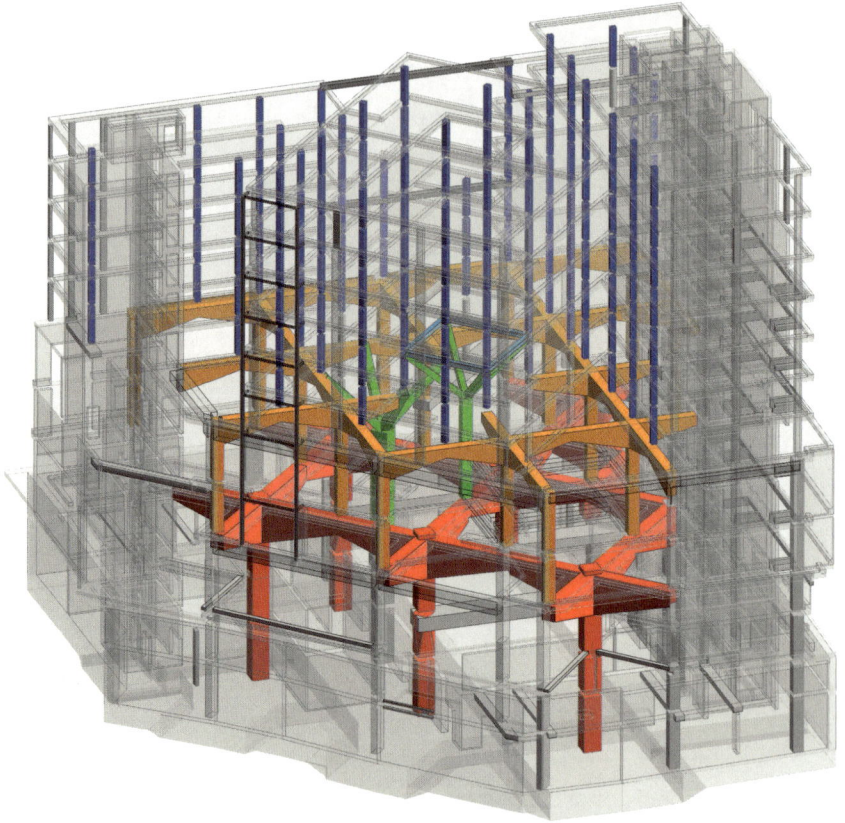

Axonometric of Structural Transfer Trees, AKT II.

immediate access to the two consecutive 'teaching floors' above. A salient feature of these floors is the provision of lecture halls on each level, positioned in such a way as to be bracketed by the structure. These halls, articulated from each other by smaller classrooms, are furnished in such a way as to conform to the so-called Harvard Lecture Theatre format, that is to say continuous benches and seats that are laid out in a u-formation to encourage cross axial exchange rather than the old-fashioned style of frontal lecturing.

At the third level, the planimetric form of the building radically changes as the pentagonal footprint of the site is broken up, as it were, into three 'blocks' of offices on each floor; a central, squarish block centred about the light-well and two rectangular side blocks served by corridors. These last are partially separated from the central block at the third floor by in-set roof terraces whereby the overall mass form assumes a more 'plastic' character.

The most evident civic aspect of this work is unquestionably the Great Hall, the monumental presence of which is emphasised by the massive reinforced concrete cantilevers which extend for some seven-and-a-half metres from the point of support where their depth appears to be virtually half the height of the space. The other key factor in terms of *civitas* is the mode and placement of the three points of entry, first the main approach from Lincoln's Inn

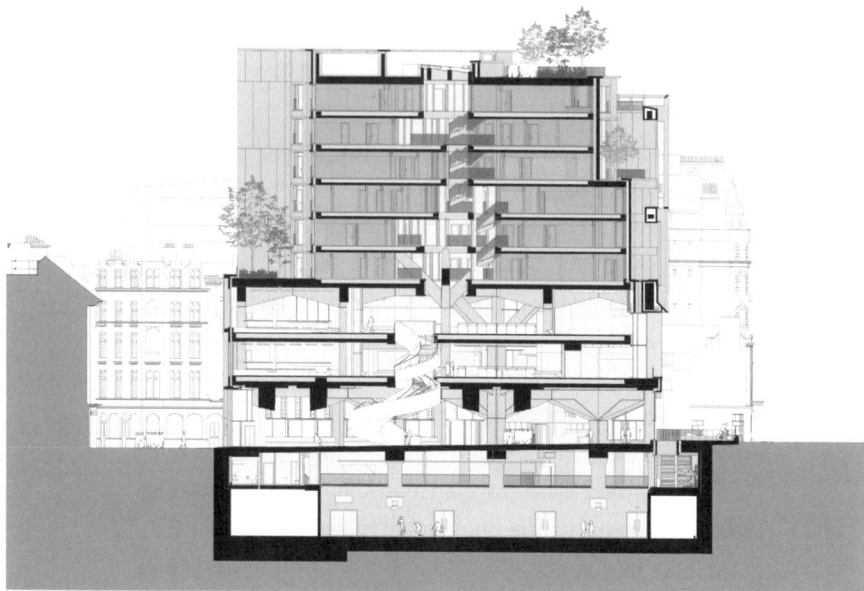

Top: Section of the Marshall Building,
Grafton Architects.

Fields, spanning over the basement bicycle storage and second, the two rear entrances, at either end of the Portsmouth Street representational façade which is equipped with continuous stone-faced benches, inside and out.

These last are accompanied by a fully glazed, steel-framed front, with a lower tier of sliding windows which when open serve to unify the implicitly collective space of the benches. This unusual feature plus the overall generosity of the space and the deep, wide-span, transfer trusses overhead, remind one of the monumental galleria of the 19th century in as much as the space within is simultaneously both a private domain and a *res publica*.

It is fitting given its honorific location that this, the last of three consecutive business schools built to the designs of Grafton Architects over the past fifteen years should evoke, however unconsciously, the genius of Sir John Soane. I am alluding to the system of wide-span, cantilevered transfer beams that roof over the Great Hall of the Marshall Building, the civic scale of which recalls the equally generous and daringly tectonic scale of Soane's Five Per Cent Office built in the Bank of England between 1818 and 1823 (see p. 96). In a similar manner the light-well cascading down through the multi-layered space above the hall recalls Soane's penchant for unexpected shafts of light entering from above.

Bottom left: View of Great Hall with terrazzo bench and sliding windows to right. Photograph by Ed Reeve.

Bottom right: View of external bench along Portsmouth St façade. Photograph by Ed Reeve.

Parallel Themes in Soane and Grafton's work, twinning architectural concerns

Deborah Saunt

Parallel Themes in Soane and Grafton's work, twinning architectural concerns

Deborah Saunt

Infrastructure is the armature that supports society, and the way it is experienced – how it communicates its values and ideas through its form – is an integral part of architecture. Both Grafton and Sir John Soane embrace this. What distinguishes them each in their approach is the way they effortlessly grasp how spaces can act simultaneously, both at an intimate as well as infrastructural scale.

Initially, one might associate infrastructure with being an immutable, top-down imposition, and less specificity related to the architecture of a single building or one's experience on the ground. Yet our infrastructure responds to evolving needs, and must be adaptable in the long term, and in good examples, it can exponentially improve our quality of life and reveal its higher purpose at the service of the greater good. However, achieving a sense of intimacy, of personal comfort at a human scale on the ground, might seem to be contradictory to the wider aims of infrastructure.

A successful combination of these qualities is evident in both the Marshall Building for the London School of

Opposite top: Soane Office, view of the interior of the Five Per Cent Office at the Bank of England, 1818-1823. © Sir John Soane's Museum, London. Photograph by Geremy Butler.

Opposite bottom: View of Great Hall at the Marshall Building. Grafton Architects. Photograph by Nick Kane.

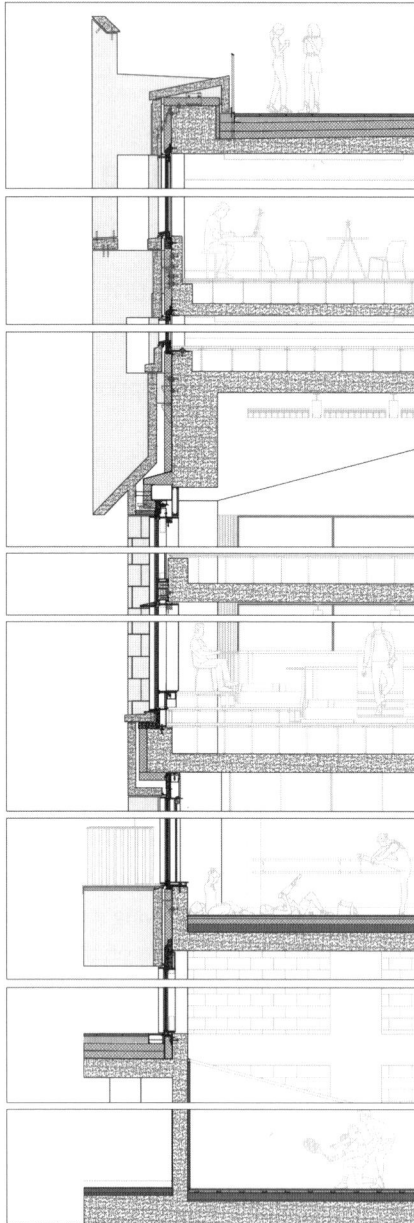

Economics (LSE) and Soane's Five Per Cent (later Colonial) Office at the Bank of England. Grafton seem to be able to magically take the tension between infrastructure and the individual and embody it in their robust juxtaposition of a raw material aesthetic with a deeply humane awareness of how spaces really feel for the people who use them. Here, education can be appreciated not only in the way the building caters for learning but also for its strategic, civic role in knowledge exchange within the wider world. Rather than just a space for learning, this building is part of society as a whole, helping to hold us all together.

The notion of community is found not just in the city status of Grafton's architecture but in the details too, which accommodate smaller needs. To bring comfort, for example, by making a subtle place of shelter on the street where a simple stone bench offers a place to rest, or meet friends, to make a private call, or just sense nature, the sun and trees around you. In both of these projects, despite the many floors of academic offices and study areas which subtly project above you, the spaces feel open and almost weightless.

An abiding conundrum in architecture always remains how to mediate the critical transitions of one continuous journey that is experienced first-hand – from outside to inside, from exposure to shelter, from public street to

Opposite: Detail section through façade to Lincoln's Inn Fields. Grafton Architects.

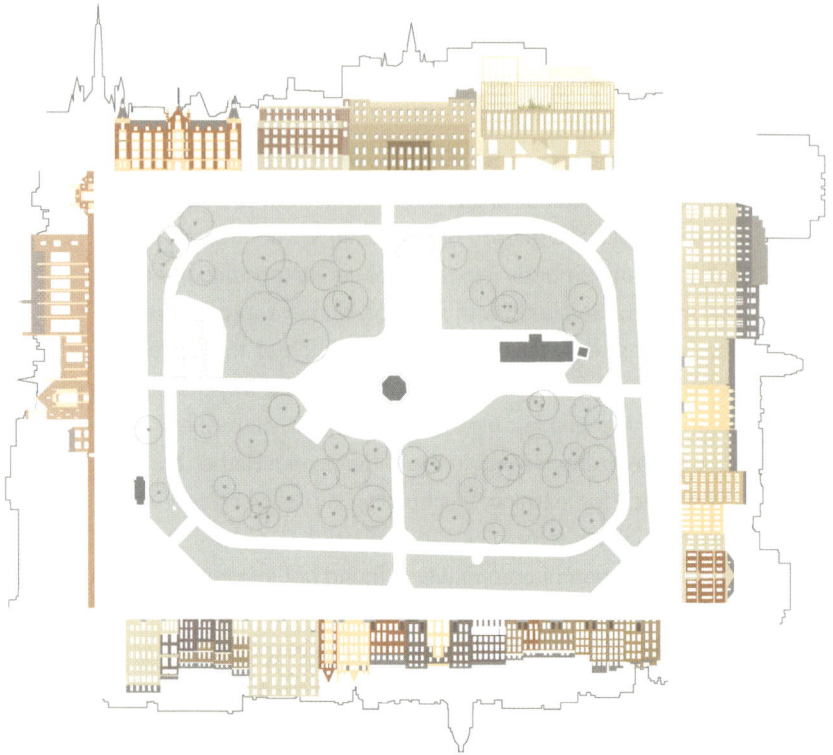

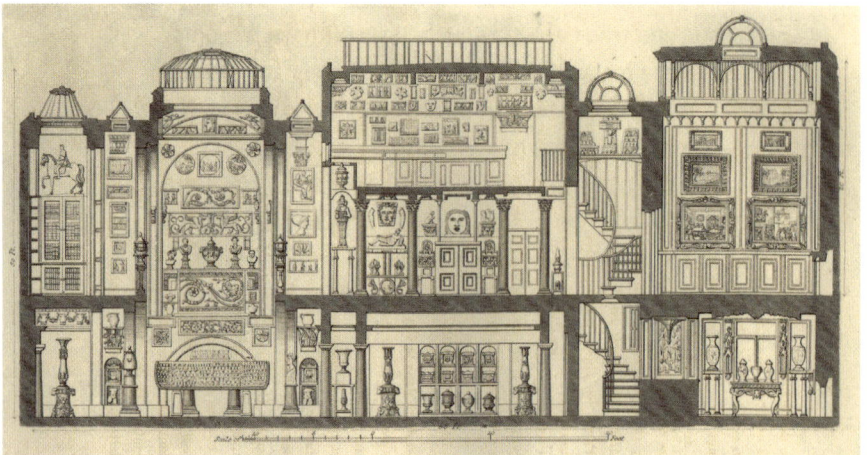

institution, into one's inner world – and grapple with the thresholds between. How can the sequences embody a set of values, at the same time as defining space for practical purposes? In Sir John Soane's Museum, likewise a place of sharing knowledge and scholarship, display and collecting coexist with a domestic setting, bringing together a hybrid environment which stretches the mind as well as focusing it.

Spatially, Lincoln's Inn Fields is a jostling interplay of styles and scales in heterogenous urban fabric, from the slightly-too-big expanse of greenery that makes this London 'square' more of a park than a formal garden, to the fragmented interplay of smaller alleys towards the medieval Inns of Court, alongside the grandiosity of 20th-century Kingsway. Below the surface, if you pause, it is socially incoherent too. Despite its unifying address, here legal pomp rubs shoulders with harried commuters, and LSE students and philanthropists share the pavement with those queuing for the soup kitchen.

Grafton's Lincoln's Inn Fields building combines delicacy and force to broker a succinct conversation with grand palazzos, porticoes and cornices. On the corner, it is part of a congregation of elements that talks to the everyday – a barber and the Old Curiosity Shop, then leading towards the individual modern blocks and appropriated older buildings that comprise the vibrant LSE.

Opposite top: Fold-out elevation of Lincoln's Inn Fields, Grafton Architects.

Opposite bottom: Section through Sir John Soane's Museum, engraving from *The Union of Architecture, Sculpture and Painting* by John Britton, 1827. © Sir John Soane's Museum, London. Photograph by Geremy Butler.

Neither Grafton's Marshall Building nor Sir John Soane's Museum accepts the notion of a façade as a single skin punctured by apertures – instead both prefer to see a building greeting the world as a layered threshold, a space in between, not a fixed point into an edifice. Firstly, we read the building's form as an urban figure, establishing its volume and placement within the contextual hierarchy. With a singular formal move at his house, Soane aggrandised his flat-fronted terraced house, one of many in the square, with a thin but somehow inhabited layer in the projecting loggia, contrasting its materials against brickwork and transforming his Museum into a prominent local landmark.

Soane's house unfolds to reveal a sequence of compressive crepuscular spaces juxtaposed with expansive tent-like enclosures, then an excavated *Wunderkammer* rising to the sunlit *piano nobile* as belvedere looking out across the park, all the while managing the interplay of several functions – school of architecture and home with collection.[1]

Across the square, Grafton provide a place of learning combined with other competing uses layered vertically from the physicality of the body in the sports centre upwards through the social public ground to the cerebral research accommodation above.

1. This was not a new idea to Soane, as his Dulwich Picture Gallery demonstrated by combining the typology of top-lit public galleries, with a mausoleum and almshouses.

Beyond creating novel typologies, the unifying concern for both Grafton and Soane is the ease with which they manage the material fact that buildings are heavy, compressive, constructed forms of social as well as spatial infrastructure that can too easily be overbearing and restrictive. Both harness building fabric and infrastructure alongside nature, light and human life. In doing so, they design with a poetic determination and a forceful delicacy, resulting in spaces where contrasting qualities can coexist and be in equipoise.

Approaching the Marshall Building, the interior sometimes hidden from view during the day, nearby trees glittering in reflections on the expanse of ground-level glazing, only the slightest hint of the dynamics inside is possible. The front door is placed at a point where, carved into the stone façade, two angles meet, and welcome you into a wide horizontal 'space between'.[2] This is where the dispersed city of students comes together in an unexpectedly open and well-lit territory, save for a few powerful concrete trees, clearly of colossal strength, supporting weighty worlds above, but without appearing to strain. Sheltering the space, and in contrast

2. As Alison and Peter Smithson described the unique characteristics of successful urban spaces that accommodated the specific patterns of human habitation associated with modernity.

to the slightly inclined floor plane, the ceiling is an inverted mineral landscape, made rhythmic by the formation of the criss-crossing tapered beams rising and falling above.

The structural tree-forms spread and lift different scale volumes; classroom, breakout spaces and offices as well as several easily accessible outdoor planted terraces. At all times light, or the promise of more light, comes from above, creating a metaphorical garden of learning, under the branches of which young people gather and learn peer to peer, and new relationships are nurtured.

A glance upwards reveals light coming from a hidden source as in a baroque church, or the work of Soane who could dematerialise space into a conversation between form, light and materiality. And Soane always designed in anticipation of the effect it would have on a person in the space at any time of day, alone or in a group, or collectively as an institution.

As in so much of Soane's work, most notably in the Bank of England, and for Grafton at UTEC in Lima, paring back structure to its essence, carving deep penetrating light shafts, overriding the entangled demands that architects have to pin down and contain within a building, both result in a remarkable humane weightlessness so that 'all that is solid melts into air'.[3]

3. Marshall Berman, *All That is Solid Melts into Air: The Experience of Modernity.* London: Verso Books, 1983.

Concept section sketch for the
Marshall Building, Grafton Architects.

Architecture of Connection

Marina Tabassum

Architecture of Connection

Marina Tabassum

'Did the world need the Fifth Symphony before
Beethoven wrote it?
Did Beethoven need it?
He desired it and the world needs it.
Desire brings new needs.'
Louis I Kahn, 1969

His house is not merely a house but a House itself –
where time, space, place, desire, passion, expression
all come together in a symphony only architecture can
create; the music of the mind.

Did the world need Sir John Soane's Museum?
He desired it and the world of architecture is richer
because of its existence.

Coming out of Holborn station walking towards
Lincoln's Inn Fields one is instantaneously aware of the
power of Sir John Soane, a passionate collector who spent
his entire life perfecting the repository of his collection.

Sir John Soane's Museum, The Dome Area and
Sepulchral Chamber with the sarcophagus of
Seti I, 2009. Photograph by Martin Clayton.

Standing in the radiance of a light-filled atrium looking down to the sarcophagus, one cannot but wonder what came first? The architecture or the art? Power of anticipation takes over and draws the curious spectator in an exploration through the carefully crafted sequence of spaces. The spirit of Sir John Soane is ever-present and it is impossible not to feel it.

Good architecture has the ability to engage in dialogue in a synchronous vibration without overwhelming the inhabitant. We call such architecture inspirational. And we, architects, are suckers for such spaces. We spend our lives trying to create architecture where nature, place, context, people all unite in a communion that transcends time. That is no easy task and clearly not for the faint-hearted. It requires a deep understanding and patience; as well as time and resistance to the instantaneous. It requires architecture to go beyond the utilitarian agenda to address the intangible, quintessential relationship of space and humanity.

Shelley McNamara and Yvonne Farrell are inspirational in that regard. They create architecture that grows from the history of the context, choreographing spaces, stitching the fabrics of the city and breathing new life into the place. Lincoln's Inn Fields, a 17th-century square, is richer because of the Marshall Building emanating the exuberance of youth both literally and figuratively. Essentially an architecture of connection, the Great Hall of the Marshall Building offers the

atmosphere of a piazza with murmuring sounds of students. The imposing tree-like structure of the transfer beams make one wonder if this has a reference to the architect Louis Kahn's narrative of the beginning of a school: 'a man under a tree, talking to a few people about a realisation he had. He did not know he was a teacher and those who listened did not know they were pupils.' One cannot ignore the power of anticipation as one climbs the sculptural spiral of the stair to

View of the Great Hall at the Marshall Building, Grafton Architects. Photograph by Ed Reeve.

reach the quiet ambiance of the common space for students, their faces glowing with the light from their computers, in a very weird way reminiscent of Soane's collection of busts beaming in daylight. The gentle curvature of the lecture hall walls adds fluidity of movement, at the same time offering a place to sit. 'Freespace' comes to mind, as in Shelley and Yvonne's reference to the Medici Palace in Florence.

Sitting against the lecture hall wall, absorbing the quietness of the atmosphere looking out on to the heart of LSE, I ponder, do architectural concerns change from one century to the next? Would Sir John Soane invite Shelley and Yvonne for a morning tea in his shallow-domed breakfast room in praise of the new addition to the Lincoln's Inn Fields? Their shared quest for the transformative power of light and space would clearly bond them together. Certain human yearnings are primordial and have not changed through time and millennia. Indeed, the agendas are expanding and investigations are becoming deeper and more complex as the demands grow in our cities. LSE is growing and consciously crafting the surrounding city fabric by encouraging an architecture of connection that not only brings together fragments of the city but also bridges the past and the present. The Marshall Building offers not only silence that prompts a dialogue of minds but also creates a new marker for London, a point of departure for planning.

Opposite top: View of Student Commons at the Marshall Building, Grafton Architects. Photograph by Ed Reeve.

Opposite bottom: Busts on display at Sir John Soane's Museum. Photograph by Gareth Gardner.

Dennis Gilbert
A selection of construction photographs

Dennis Gilbert (1951–2021) photographed the Marshall Building while it was under construction in July of 2020, capturing the concrete branch structures and helical stair before the installation of linings, metalwork and other finishes.

Previous page: View of Helical Stair from First
Floor to Second Floor with 'Concrete Tree' above.
© Dennis Gilbert/VIEW.
Above: View of from Ground Floor of 'Concrete
Tree' stretching up to the underside of the third
floor slab. © Dennis Gilbert/VIEW.

Dennis Gilbert

View of Helical Stair from Ground Floor.
© Dennis Gilbert/VIEW.

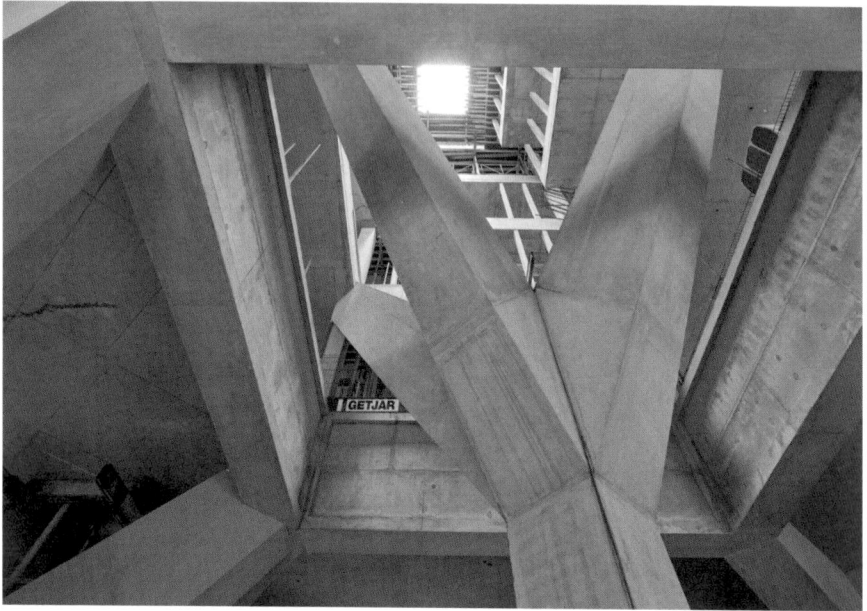

Above: View of 'Concrete Tree' at third floor branching up into void at fourth floor.
© Dennis Gilbert/VIEW.
Opposite: View of Helical Stair and 'Concrete Branch Beams' beyond.
© Dennis Gilbert/VIEW.

Following spread, left: View of 'Concrete Tree' passing through void at first floor.
© Dennis Gilbert/VIEW.
Following spread, right: View across second floor through 'Concrete Trees'.
© Dennis Gilbert/VIEW.

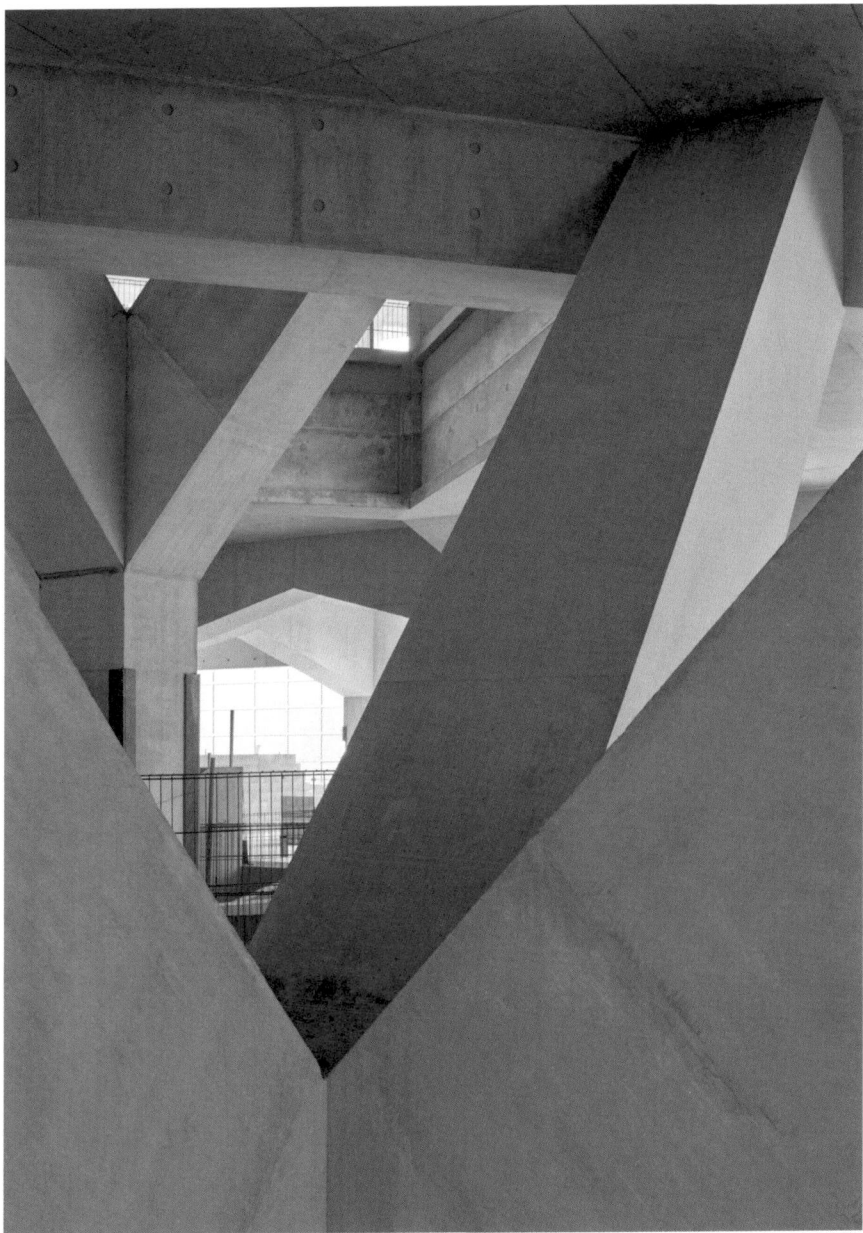

Contributors

Bruce Boucher, Deborah Loeb Brice Director of Sir John Soane's Museum, is an art historian and curator specialising in Renaissance and Baroque sculpture and architecture. He is professor emeritus at University College London, where he taught for over 20 years, and has published a number of books. Before joining the Soane, Bruce was Director of the Fralin Museum of Art at the University of Virginia, which followed a role as Curator and Head of European Sculpture, Decorative Arts, and Ancient Art at the Art Institute, Chicago. He is former President of the Board of the Center for Palladian Studies in America and currently a Fellow of the Society of Antiquaries.

Grafton Architects headed by the 2020 Pritzker Prize laureates, Yvonne Farrell and Shelley McNamara, is the recent winner of the RIBA Gold Medal (2020), the RIBA Stirling Prize (2021) and the Mies van der Rohe Award (2022).

Kenneth Frampton is an architect and historian and is Ware Professor Emeritus at the Graduate School of Architecture, Planning, and Preservation at Columbia University.

Deborah Saunt is an architect and one of the founding directors of DSDHA. She has held academic appointments at Yale School of Architecture, Universidad de Navarra, École Polytechnique Fédérale de Lausanne and the University of Cambridge and helped found the London School of Architecture in 2015.

Marina Tabassum is Founder and Principal Architect of Marina Tabassum Architects MTA in Dhaka and is a pioneer of what she describes as 'the architecture of relevance'. She is Visiting Professor at BRAC University in Dhaka and Director of Academic Program at Bengal Institute for Architecture. Tabassum was awarded the Soane Medal in 2021.

Louise Stewart is an art and architectural historian and Head of Exhibitions at Sir John Soane's Museum, London.

Dennis Gilbert (1951–2021) was a leading architectural photographer, founder of the photographic archive VIEW Pictures and an Honorary Fellow of the RIBA, elected in 2005.

Editorial Team

Sir John Soane's Museum
Louise Stewart
Erin McKellar
Sue Palmer
Helen Dorey
Nathan Emery

Grafton Architects
Yvonne Farrell
Shelley McNamara
Ger Carty
David Healy
Alanah Doyle
James Rossa O'Hare

Pages for Sketching

2 worlds?

3 basements?